Creating Young Expert Learners

Other Redleaf Press books by Marla J. Lohmann

Positive Behavior Interventions and Supports for Preschool and Kindergarten

Creating Young Expert Learners

Universal Design for Learning in
Preschool and Kindergarten

Marla J. Lohmann, PhD

www.redleafpress.org
800-423-8309

Published by Redleaf Press
10 Yorkton Court
St. Paul, MN 55117
www.redleafpress.org

First edition 2023
Cover design by Louise OFarrell
Cover photograph by FatCamera/iStock
Interior design by Wendy Holdman
Typeset in Warnock Pro, Acumin Pro, and Brix Slab
Printed in the United States of America
30 29 28 27 26 25 24 23   1 2 3 4 5 6 7 8

Library of Congress Cataloging-in-Publication Data
Names: Lohmann, Marla J., author.
Title: Creating young expert learners : universal design for learning in preschool and
    kindergarten / by Marla J. Lohmann.
Description: First edition. | St. Paul, MN : Redleaf Press, 2023. | Includes bibliographical
    references and index. | Summary: "This book includes a theoretical introduction to
    the concept of Universal Design for Learning (UDL) as it applies to young children, as
    well as practical examples of common early childhood learning units designed within a
    UDL framework. Vignettes and examples help early childhood educators connect the
    theory to practice, and sample learning units are included for teachers to use in their
    own classrooms"— Provided by publisher.
Identifiers: LCCN 2022030136 (print) | LCCN 2022030137 (ebook) |
    ISBN 9781605547596 (paperback) | ISBN 9781605547602 (ebook)
Subjects: LCSH: Education, Preschool. | Kindergarten. | Instructional systems—Design. |
    Individualized instruction. | Cognitive styles.
Classification: LCC LB1140.2 .L588 2023 (print) | LCC LB1140.2 (ebook) |
    DDC 372.21—dc23/eng/20220810
LC record available at https://lccn.loc.gov/2022030136
LC ebook record available at https://lccn.loc.gov/2022030137

Printed on acid-free paper

This book is dedicated to the preschool and kindergarten teachers
who work hard every day to ensure success for ALL learners.
Thank you for your passion, dedication, and expertise!

Contents

Acknowledgments

I would like to thank everyone who helped make this book a reality. First, I want to thank my family. To Mark, Abigail, Charlotte, Esther, and Abraham—thank you for believing in me and supporting my dreams. I am beyond blessed to have the five of you as my family! Maybe one day I will write a book about dragons and fairies for you.

Next I would like to thank my professional colleagues who have helped me grow in my own knowledge of effective instruction for young children. To Dr. Ariane Gauvreau and Dr. Kate Hovey—thank you for being my coauthors on several articles related to Universal Design for Learning (UDL) in preschool. By working with you, I have learned so much about how this framework enhances learning for young children. To Dr. Kathy Boothe, Dr. Ruby Owiny, and Dr. Jennifer Walker—thank you for collaborating with me on countless projects related to UDL! I look forward to years of continued partnership with all of you.

Additionally, thank you to the early childhood teachers who inspire me every day. I would especially like to thank Erika Alvis, Mindy Tipton, Ann Rennie, and Kristin Roberts. Talking to each of you and spending time in your classrooms helps me stay focused on the *why* of this work. Each of you is a gifted teacher, and I am honored to know you.

Finally, I want to thank the folks at Redleaf Press for assisting me in bringing my book dreams to reality. I especially want to thank Melissa York. Melissa—I love working with you! I always look forward to Zoom conversations with you, and your feedback makes me a much better writer. Thank you for supporting me and for supporting young children and their teachers.

Introduction

When I was a little girl, I loved to play school. I spent hours in my bedroom teaching my dolls and my stuffed animals. I read books to them, created hands-on learning activities for them, and emulated much of what I saw my own teachers doing. I distinctly remember that Brown Bear needed a little extra support in reading and that Strawberry Shortcake often required reminders to pay attention while I was talking. Even in that early make-believe classroom, I understood that no two children are identical and that being a successful teacher requires providing instruction that is adaptable for all learners.

In every classroom where I have taught (my pretend childhood classroom, a toddler classroom, multiple special education classrooms, and graduate school courses), I have encountered wide variability in student needs, interests, and abilities. As a teacher, I want to ensure that I provide instruction and supports to meet these needs, and that all of my students have the tools they need to succeed. That is where Universal Design for Learning (UDL) comes in. The UDL framework guides you to proactively design your instruction so that it meets the needs of any student who may walk into your classroom.

I first learned about UDL about eight years ago when I was asked to teach a graduate course on the topic. As soon as I started researching, I instantly grew excited about UDL's potential. CAST (formerly Center for Applied Special Technology) invented the term *Universal Design for Learning*, and some of the seminal and most influential work on the topic comes from this group. As I learned more about UDL, I realized that I had instinctively always used this framework to some extent in my classrooms. But as I have learned more and practiced UDL implementation, my skills have grown over the years. I still have a lot of learning to do and am excited to continue growing my knowledge of UDL.

As a teacher who is reading this book, you are constantly seeking to better support the needs of all learners in your classroom. I suspect you hope to gain some ideas not only to help young children who are struggling in your classroom but also to enhance the learning of the children who are meeting or exceeding developmental expectations. You may be reading this book alone or with others in a book study. Regardless of why or how you have come to read this book, I want to start by thanking you for choosing this book and for making the learning of the children in your classroom a priority. The work you do every day is amazing, and I am thankful for dedicated and motivated teachers like you!

This book includes six chapters that will expand your knowledge about the Universal Design for Learning framework in the preschool and kindergarten classroom.

Chapter 1 provides an overview of the UDL framework as it applies to early childhood classrooms. In this chapter, I introduce you to the concept of using multiple means of engagement, representation, and action and expression to support the learning needs of all young children in the classroom.

Chapter 2 offers a focused look at using multiple means of engagement with young children. This chapter presents ways to support young children in becoming interested and motivated learners in your classroom and outside in the world.

Chapter 3 talks about using multiple means of representation to provide instruction that meets the learning preferences of all young children. It explores a variety of teaching techniques and tools that you can use when designing instruction for your classroom.

Chapter 4 continues the conversation with a focus on providing multiple means of action and expression so that young children can show you what they know. This chapter will aid you as you design a variety of authentic assessments.

Chapter 5 pulls together the three UDL principles and offers you some simple strategies for designing lessons and learning units to meet the needs of all young children in your classroom.

In chapter 6, I conclude the book with a recap of the first five chapters. I offer suggestions for using the UDL framework to support your collaborations with families and other professionals and to guide your own teacher professional development.

After chapter 6 follows a discussion guide that you can complete alone or with colleagues as you read this book.

www.redleafpress
.org/cyl/D-Q.pdf

I challenge you to take your time as you read and consider how you can implement the ideas from each section before moving on to the next. While you can likely read the entire book in one sitting, I suggest reading a chapter and spending time implementing what you are learning before moving on to the next chapter. And if you are reading this book with others, take time between chapters to work through the discussion questions and share how you each are implementing the UDL framework in your own classrooms. As you read through the book, please reach out to me via Twitter (@MarlaLohmann) with any questions or thoughts. I am hoping to learn even more about UDL from your experiences with this book. Let's get started with our adventure together!

Young Expert Learners: Who Are They and How Do We Support Their Development?

Miss Smith has been teaching in an inclusive kindergarten classroom for ten years, and she realizes that every year there has been increasing variability in the children. When she first began teaching, her students mostly lived in her neighborhood and were white and middle class, like her, and the children with disabilities attended a different school. Each year, she has taught more and more children with disabilities as well as children from a variety of cultural backgrounds and with diverse family structures. Each year, Miss Smith's skills have grown and she has worked to improve her own abilities to meet the needs of all learners. She knows that every child has different needs that must be met to ensure their success. But even with her current knowledge, Miss Smith feels that she can do more to ensure that all children are learning, and she is looking for a system to help her in this endeavor.

Like Miss Smith, your classroom includes young children with diverse strengths, needs, interests, and personalities. The children in your class come from a variety of backgrounds and family structures with a range of typical and less typical skills and developmental levels. Meeting everyone's needs can be challenging.

You may be asking yourself how one teacher can possibly do it all. How can you ensure that their academic, social, emotional, behavioral, and self-care needs are all met? There are only eight-ish hours in your school day, and resources are limited. Well, I have excellent news for you! While you can't "do it all," there is a way to ensure that the needs of every child in your classroom are met. The answer is Universal Design for Learning, known as UDL.

Terminology for Discussing Disabilities

There is debate over the preferred terminology to use when discussing disabilities. Some people choose to use person-first language, such as "boy with an intellectual disability" or "child with visual impairment." Those who make this choice do so because they want to emphasize that the child is first a person and that the disability is one characteristic of that person. Other people use identity-first language, such as "Deaf girl" or "autistic child," as this verbiage signifies that the disability is a critical part of the person's identity and reinforces the idea that disabilities are not something to hide or be ashamed of. Whenever possible, we should ask the individual with the disability which they prefer. If this is not possible, you as a teacher should make the decision that is most appropriate for the situation. In this book, I have chosen to use person-first language as I want to focus on the fact that every child in our classrooms is first a child.

AN EQUITY-BASED APPROACH

UDL is a framework for designing classroom instruction that focuses on meeting diverse needs and ensuring an equitable learning experience for all children. Recent events have brought a variety of concerns to the surface. The COVID pandemic and an increased awareness of racial injustices and the impacts of socioeconomic status have led to discussions within the field of education about how we can better address inequalities. We know that all children do not come to school with the same background and experiences. Children's experiences before they begin school, as well as their experiences outside of the school setting, have a significant impact on their ability to access learning and to succeed in the classroom. Inequalities affect children at a young age; in fact, one study indicates that children from low-income backgrounds tend to have social and language delays at nine months of age (Halle et al. 2009). Over time gaps get larger, and the negative outcomes can be seen in language development, reading skills, academic test scores, school suspensions and expulsions, and graduation rates (Howard 2015). It is vital that, as teachers, we understand the effects of societal inequality and consider equity in our lesson planning and in our daily interactions with children so that we can help guide all learners to better outcomes.

Before we can do that, we must understand the term *equity*. *Equity* and *equality* are not synonyms. The term *equality* indicates that we are providing the exact same supports to every learner, regardless of their individual needs. This is not good practice and does not meet the needs of many learners in our classrooms. Think of it this way: I am the mom of four children. If I approached parenting from an equality perspective, I would purchase size 3 shoes for each child, buy them each Magic Tree House books to read, and enroll each of them in soccer camp. Of course, this would not meet each child's needs and interests—only one of them has size 3 feet, my oldest two children are too old for Magic Tree House, and my youngest cannot yet read but is the only one who likes soccer. Parenting from an equality perspective would lead to a lot of frustration. Similarly, if we approach classroom instruction from an equality perspective, we won't get our desired results.

Conversely, an equity-minded approach to classroom instruction means that we aim to remove barriers and ensure that each child's needs are met. This would mean that, as a parent, I am buying four different sizes of shoes, providing a variety of books, and enrolling my children in their own extracurricular activities. It means that, as a teacher, I recognize the individuality of my students and meet each of them where they are. My end goal for each child is individual success, but I know they will need different supports to be successful and that success will look different for each child.

It is important to note that as I am writing this book in 2022, CAST, the originator of UDL, is working to better address equity through the framework. CAST recently requested input from stakeholders, and changes or additions to the UDL framework may occur as a result of this work. It is encouraging to see how they are explicitly working to ensure that UDL offers equity for all learners, and I am excited to see what changes they make.

THE PRINCIPLES OF UDL

Universal Design for Learning has three primary principles: multiple means of engagement, multiple means of representation, and multiple means of action and expression. Together these three principles ensure that we offer the supports our students need to succeed, specifically in the areas of motivation, instruction, and demonstration of children's knowledge. Later chapters discuss each of these principles in depth, but for now, here is a quick overview.

Multiple means of engagement refers to the ways in which we systematically ensure that young children are motivated and engaged in the learning activities in our classroom (Lohmann, Hovey, and Gauvreau 2018). Multiple means of representation encompasses the various ways in which we teach the content in our classroom (Gauvreau, Lohmann, and Hovey 2019). Finally, multiple means of action and expression indicates that we offer different ways to evaluate the learning of young children and their mastery of developmentally appropriate skills (Glass, Meyer, and Rose 2013). CAST has aligned checkpoints with each of these three principles; the checkpoints are presented in the chapters related to each principle. You will note as you read the book that I have not provided examples for how to meet every checkpoint. I want to emphasize that the best way to implement any new framework, including UDL, in your classroom is to start small. Begin with one small thing and master that before adding a second small thing. In this book, I present simple changes or ideas that you can implement in your classroom.

My favorite place to continue learning the basics (and intricacies) of Universal Design for Learning is the CAST website. It offers visuals to help users understand the concept of UDL broadly as well as blog posts and webinars that discuss specific issues related to UDL for all ages, from early childhood through graduate school. In addition, Katie Novak has a fantastic blog that offers practical examples of UDL, especially as it applies in the K–12 classroom.

Figure 1.1 offers a list of additional resources that I highly recommend for learning more about Universal Design for Learning in the school setting. These resources are not specific to early childhood, but they will get you started thinking more deeply about the framework as you continue reading this book.

Figure 1.1

Recommended Resources for Learning about Universal Design for Learning

Online Articles

Amanda Morin, "Universal Design for Learning (UDL): What You Need to Know." Reading Rockets, 2021. www.readingrockets.org/article/universal-design -learning-udl-what-you-need-know.

Allison Posey, "Universal Design for Learning (UDL): A Teacher's Guide." Understood.org. www.understood.org/articles/en/understanding-universal -design-for-learning.

Videos

CAST, *UDL at a Glance*, January 6, 2010, 4:36. www.youtube.com/watch?v= bDvKnYog6e4.

National Center on Universal Design for Learning, *The UDL Guidelines*, March 17, 2010, 6:20. www.youtube.com/watch?v=rfsx3DGpv50.

Michael Nesmith, *Why We Need Universal Design*. TedXTalks, October 13, 2016, 10:29. www.youtube.com/watch?v=bVdPNWMGyZY.

Novak Educational Consulting, *What Is UDL?*, January 8, 2021, 3:21. www.youtube.com /watch?v=eYN-qrKIIYI.

Books

Andratesha Fritzgerald, *Antiracism and Universal Design for Learning: Building Expressways to Success* (Wakefield, MA: CAST Professional Publishing, 2020).

Anne Meyer, David H. Rose, and David Gordon, *Universal Design for Learning: Theory and Practice* (Wakefield, MA: CAST Professional Publishing, 2014).

Wendy W. Murawski and Kathy Lynn Scott, eds., *What Really Works with Universal Design for Learning* (Thousand Oaks, CA: Corwin Press, 2019).

Katie Novak, *UDL Now! A Teacher's Guide to Applying Universal Design for Learning*, 3rd ed. (Wakefield, MA: CAST Professional Publishing, 2022).

Online Learning Module

IRIS Center. *Universal Design for Learning: Creating a Learning Environment That Challenges and Engages All Students*, 2021. https://iris.peabody.vanderbilt.edu/module /udl.

THE ORIGIN OF UNIVERSALLY DESIGNED SUPPORTS

The concept of universal design first came from the field of architecture, as professionals began designing and building structures that were accessible to everyone. This drive for making buildings accessible happened in part because soldiers returned from the world wars with lifelong injuries that limited their movement at the same time as people began living longer and therefore developed more age-related disabilities (Centre for Excellence in Universal Design 2020). Today the use of universal design ensures that structures meet the requirements under the Americans with Disabilities Act and Section 504 of the Rehabilitation Act (Simmons 2020).

While universally designed structures were specifically meant to ensure access for persons with disabilities, these modifications often help everyone. Let's consider wheelchair ramps. They ensure that people using wheelchairs can get into buildings, but many others also use the ramps. As a mom, I have relied heavily on wheelchair ramps while pushing strollers or wagons. Wheelchair ramps were not designed for me, but I certainly use them and benefit from their existence. Similarly, some of my university students rely heavily on closed captioning for the videos I post in my courses even if they do not have any hearing loss. Because they are often doing their homework in the same room as their children, who are also doing homework or playing, they need to be able to hear what is going on around them. Closed captioning allows them to keep their ears open to the needs of their families while still completing their work for my course.

UDL with Other Frameworks

For those of you working in schools that are using Multi-Tiered Systems of Support (MTSS), which includes Response to Intervention (RtI) and Positive Behavior Interventions and Supports (PBIS), the UDL framework is part of a solid Tier 1 that focuses on effective instruction for all learners (Juergensen and Thomas 2019). This graphic offers a basic visual of UDL as it fits in the MTSS framework.

```
            Tier 3
        Individualized
           supports
          for a small
        number of learners


            Tier 2
      Small-group supports
         for some learners


            Tier 1
   Universal supports for all learners
   Universal Design for Learning
```

DON'T WE ALREADY DO THIS?

As you have read the past few sections, you may have thought something like, "I already do this. I have supports in my classroom to ensure that everyone's needs are met, and I teach using a variety of tools." This sentiment is correct. Most of the early childhood teachers I know teach using multiple means of representation and multiple means of action and expression. They also engage learners in a variety of ways. This is amazing and reflects your strong teaching skills. The difference between what occurs in most early childhood classrooms and implementing the UDL framework is the intentionality with which you develop your instruction. A universally designed learning environment is put together in a very proactive and intentional manner and is created to support any learner who may walk into your classroom, not just those who are already there.

During my first year as a public school teacher, I had several students show up in my classroom with no notice. For example, one day the school secretary walked a child into my room and said, "Rafael's mother just registered him for school here, and he is assigned to your class, starting immediately." I didn't know about UDL back then, but I certainly wish I had! Rafael was an English-language learner and needed instruction provided in Spanish. I am fluent in Spanish, and I was teaching in a bilingual school, but I had set up my classroom fully in English because there were no Spanish speakers in my class on the first day of school. When students such as Rafael have been unexpectedly placed in my classroom, I have had to scramble to identify and provide the supports they needed. If my classroom had been designed using the UDL framework, I would have already had those supports available for all learners and I would not have had to scramble.

PROACTIVE VERSUS REACTIVE INSTRUCTION

As a special education teacher, my expertise has been designing and implementing interventions that meet the learning and behavior needs of specific children. This is important and will always be necessary. But these individualized interventions must be paired with proactive planning for all learners. When we adapt instructions and provide accommodations based on individual children's needs, we are responding reactively. It means the student may have to wait for us to provide the support needed—and it means that we are constantly creating and developing new supports. When we teach from a UDL framework, we design our class instruction to consider the *potential* needs children might have. We want our classroom to meet the needs of anyone who may attend on any given day.

To be clear, though, it is critical that we continue to differentiate instruction to meet the needs of all children, especially those with disabilities. If we have any children with disabilities in our classrooms who have an Individualized Family Service Plan (IFSP) or an Individualized Education Program (IEP), we are legally mandated to differentiate. I am not advocating that you stop differentiating instruction. I want you to be both a proactive and a reactive teacher. A proactive UDL approach does not replace differentiation; the two work together to ensure that all children's needs are met. And while both are critical for classroom success, this book is focused on the proactive use of UDL.

IDEA

Under the Individuals with Disabilities Education Act (IDEA), children with disabilities in the United States receive individualized instructions and supports to ensure that they can access developmentally appropriate learning, including academic, behavioral, and social instruction. For children from birth to their third birthday, these supports are provided under Part C of IDEA and are outlined in the IFSP. Depending on your state, the specific services provided may be offered through a school district, community agency, private providers, or some other organization. The IFSP is focused on ensuring the family as a whole has the supports needed that will lead to the child's success. For children ages 3–21, these services and supports are identified in an IEP and provided through the local school district. The IEP is focused on meeting the child's needs, but families are vital members of the IEP team.

WHAT ARE EXPERT LEARNERS?

Now that you understand the basics of the UDL framework, you may be wondering about the end goal. As teachers, our goal is always related to the long-term success of the students in our classroom. We want the children we teach to become successful adults, remembering that success is different for each of us. When we design our classroom following a UDL framework, we are supporting this long-term goal by helping children become expert learners. CAST (2018) describes expert learners as people who are "purposeful, motivated, resourceful, knowledgeable, strategic, and goal-directed." That might sound like a lot, but I firmly believe becoming an expert learner is an attainable goal for anyone.

In its most basic form, an expert learner is a person who takes charge of their own learning and knows what they need in order to learn. You are demonstrating your own expert learning skills as a teacher when you choose to grow your own skills and read a book on UDL. You have likely chosen to read a book because you know that you learn well from books, you prefer reading, or this method of learning fits best in your schedule. But you could have chosen to learn about UDL from watching a webinar or attending a conference (and you may choose multiple ways to learn, like reading this book and viewing a webinar too). When you choose the methods you prefer for learning, you are using your skills as an expert learner.

Similarly, we want all children to become expert learners. In the early childhood years, they need a lot of ongoing support from the adults in their lives to do this. When we give them the opportunity to learn content through a variety of methods and show us in different ways what they know, we help them explore what it means to be a learner. When we allow children to discover supports that may aid their learning, we help them begin learning how to advocate for themselves. By using UDL in preschool and kindergarten classrooms, we are supporting their development in becoming lifelong expert learners.

UDL AS A DEVELOPMENTALLY APPROPRIATE PRACTICE

Early childhood classrooms often follow the National Association for the Education of Young Children (NAEYC) Developmentally Appropriate Practice (DAP) guidelines. If your school is NAEYC accredited or your instruction is informed by NAEYC recommendations, you are likely now asking yourself where UDL falls into DAP. In short, UDL is a developmentally appropriate practice.

In 2009 NAEYC and the Council for Exceptional Children Division for Early Childhood (DEC) published a joint position statement on inclusion in early childhood classrooms. In the document, they identify that an early childhood program can be considered as inclusive if the key features of "access, participation, and supports" are present (DEC and NAEYC 2009, 2). They explicitly note that the use of a UDL framework helps to ensure that all children have access to learning in the inclusive classroom. This idea of access can be seen in multiple ways in the DAP guidelines. In addition, the *Professional Standards and Competencies for Early Childhood Educators* established by NAEYC (2020) outlines skills that align with UDL and specifically mention UDL in competency 4c. Figure 1.2 offers a list of DAP guidelines and teacher competencies that are supported when early childhood teachers use a UDL framework in their classrooms.

Figure 1.2

Universal Design for Learning and NAEYC DAP and Professional Standards

	DAP or Standard	Connection to UDL
Developmentally Appropriate Practices	1B. Relationships	One way that early childhood teachers provide multiple means of engagement is through building intentional relationships with all children in the classroom and supporting young children in building relationships with their peers.
	1E. Psychological safety	By offering multiple means of engagement, early childhood teachers ensure that children feel welcomed in the classroom and valued for their unique contributions to the classroom.
	3A. Observation, documentation, and assessment	Through the UDL principle of multiple means of action and expression, early childhood teachers intentionally select a variety of assessment tools that provide a comprehensive understanding of children's learning and development.
	3D. Responsive assessment	When using the UDL framework, early childhood teachers select a variety of assessments that are appropriate for the content being assessed and the children who are currently in the classroom (or may be in the future).
	4B. Meaningful learning experiences	Through the UDL principles of multiple means of engagement and multiple means of representation, early childhood teachers provide a variety of ways to support all learners, with a specific emphasis on the unique characteristics of each child.
	4C. Comprehensive curriculum	The three UDL principles ensure that the early childhood curriculum offers a variety of ways for all children to access and participate in learning. In addition, the description for this DAP specifically notes the use of UDL.
	4G. Learning formats and contexts	The UDL principle of multiple means of representation focuses on using various formats to teach content in the early childhood classroom.
	4H. Differentiation of instructional approaches	Each of the three UDL principles ensures that children's unique characteristics and needs are reflected in the classroom curriculum, including instruction and assessment.
	5D. Meaningful connections	Each of the three UDL principles offers ways to connect new learning to children's personal experiences and previous classroom instruction.

	DAP or Standard	Connection to UDL
Professional Standards and Competencies	3b. Types of assessments	When teachers include multiple means of action and expression, they use a variety of assessment types to better understand children's learning.
	4a. Supportive relationships and interactions	One way that early childhood teachers provide multiple means of engagement is through building intentional relationships with all children in the classroom.
	4b. Responsive teaching skills	The three principles of UDL are designed to ensure that classroom instruction is proactively responsive to the needs of all learners.
	4c. Developmentally appropriate, culturally and linguistically relevant, antibias, evidence-based teaching skills and strategies that reflect the principles of Universal Design for Learning	When early childhood teachers use the UDL framework, they offer multiple means of engagement, representation, and action and expression that ensure the needs of all learners are met.

National Association for the Education of Young Children 2022.

In the twenty-first century, the concepts of ensuring access to learning and using UDL have been noted in a variety of NAEYC publications as a means of supporting the learning of all children in early childhood classrooms. In a 2006 article published in *Beyond the Journal*, NAEYC's online companion to its print journal, the authors note the importance of universally designed instructional planning for ensuring learning and participation in the early childhood classroom (Conn-Powers et al. 2006). At the time of this writing, the most recent standards for early childhood educators note the importance of ensuring that young children "have equitable access to high-quality learning and care environments" (NAEYC 2020, 9).

UDL AS A RECOMMENDED PRACTICE

In addition to NAEYC guidelines, early childhood classrooms that support young children with disabilities are also often guided by the Council for Exceptional Children Division for Early Childhood (DEC) Recommended Practices (RPs). The RPs are not meant to replace NAEYC's DAP but instead work alongside to ensure that the specific needs of children with disabilities are met in the inclusive classroom (Division for Early Childhood 2014). The use of the UDL framework is explicitly noted in RP E2, which states that practitioners consider Universal Design for Learning principles to create accessible environments. In addition, the use of UDL supports the implementation of many RPs as indicated in figure 1.3.

Figure 1.3

Universal Design for Learning and DEC Recommend Practices

Recommended Practice	Connection to UDL
A3. Practitioners use assessment materials and strategies that are appropriate for the child's age and level of development and accommodate the child's sensory, physical, communication, cultural, linguistic, social, and emotional characteristics.	Within the UDL principle of multiple means of action and expression, early childhood teachers use a variety of assessment tools that take into account young children's individual characteristics and needs. The use of these tools provides teachers with a comprehensive understanding of children's development and learning.
A6. Practitioners use a variety of methods, including observation and interviews, to gather assessment information from multiple sources, including the child's family and other significant individuals in the child's life.	The UDL principle of multiple means of action and expression focuses on using a variety of tools and strategies to assess the learning and development of young children.
E6. Practitioners create environments that provide opportunities for movement and regular physical activity to maintain or improve fitness, wellness, and development across domains.	Guideline 4 under the UDL principle of multiple means of action and expression explicitly notes the importance of providing opportunities for children to engage in physical movement while learning.
INS4. Practitioners plan for and provide the level of support, accommodations, and adaptations needed for the child to access, participate, and learn within and across activities and routines.	Each of the three UDL principles focuses on offering a variety of supports and strategies that are proactively designed to support and accommodate the needs of young children in the classroom.

Division for Early Childhood 2014.

STARTING SMALL

I don't want you to feel overwhelmed as you read this book and think about using UDL in your classroom. The UDL framework can be intimidating, but it does not need to be. As you begin to use the framework to make changes in your classroom, start small, with just one change or idea. Once that becomes comfortable and you can do it fairly easily, add one more idea. Master that before adding a third. Adjusting your instruction slowly will make UDL implementation more doable and help ensure your success.

In the book *UDL Now!*, UDL expert Katie Novak compares the Universal Design for Learning framework to hosting a dinner party in which you serve a taco bar. By offering a variety of options and allowing each guest to personalize their meal with food they like and that meets their own dietary restrictions, you can ensure that everyone's needs are met.

Because I *love* coffee, my personal spin on this metaphor is that UDL is like the coffee bar I have always dreamed of having in my home for guests, since people of all ages with a variety of drink preferences frequent our home on a regular basis. I picture a gorgeous table with an array of coffee cups: large ceramic mugs in bright colors, small teacups on saucers, stainless steel mugs, and paper cups with lids. The table has freshly brewed light roast, medium roast, dark roast, and decaf coffees. There is hot water and tea bags, hot chocolate, and apple cider. Once my visitors have selected their hot drink base, there are myriad options for what guests can put in their cups—flavored syrups, steamed and cold milks of many types, and oodles of toppings. Every person who walks in the door is invited to grab a cup and build their dream hot drink—and come back for seconds.

I myself cozy up with the largest ceramic coffee mug and fill it with light roast coffee, steamed almond milk, crème brûlée syrup, and a few chocolate shavings on top. My husband would have a stainless steel mug with medium roast and nothing else. My son would probably have a mug full of whipped cream! Everyone who came into the house could have a drink that would meet their needs and make them smile. I would not have to plan a different beverage for every guest because my hot drink bar would already include what the people I love might enjoy. This is UDL—proactively planning for everyone's needs and preferences to provide instruction for all learners.

And now that I have coffee on my mind, I suggest we go grab ourselves our favorite hot drinks and meet back here soon to keep talking about supporting the needs of young children through UDL.

Multiple Means of Engagement: A Proactive Approach to Engaging and Motivating Young Learners

Mr. Nkosi is in his first year as a teacher in a Head Start preschool classroom. He has been working hard to use everything he learned in his teacher preparation program to support the learning and development of each child in his classroom. But several boys never seem to pay attention and are not meeting the expected developmental targets for three-year-olds. During circle time, the boys often roll around on the floor or point finger guns at one another. And during table activities, the boys get out of their seats frequently and often do not complete the assigned tasks. Mr. Nkosi is feeling frustrated and looking for a way to better support these boys as well as any other student who may enter his classroom this year or in coming years.

Like Mr. Nkosi, you may have children in your classroom who do not seem engaged in the learning, appear unmotivated, or often go off-task. This is a common issue in all classrooms, regardless of the age or developmental level of the students. This is even a challenge in the graduate-level college classroom! Even with the coolest lessons and interactive activities, children cannot learn if they are not paying attention and are not engaged. To ensure that these children benefit from our instruction, we need to explicitly create an engaging learning environment for all young children. We can do this by beginning with the UDL principle of multiple means of engagement. In the last chapter, I talked about the importance of starting small with UDL implementation and selecting one idea to implement and master first. I recommend that teachers begin with the principle of multiple means of engagement, select one strategy, and then slowly add more ways to motivate young children.

A Quick Refresher

The Universal Design for Learning framework includes three principles: multiple means of engagement, multiple means of representation, and multiple means of action and expression. These UDL principles ensure that we use a variety of methods and tools to motivate learners, teach instructional content, and assess the learning and development of young children.

One of my other passions in addition to UDL is classroom behavior management. When I talk to teachers about challenging behaviors, I first ask about children's learning needs and how they are being met. When there is a mismatch between children's learning needs and our instruction, we often see unwanted behaviors. While the entire UDL framework can help address this mismatch, it really starts with offering multiple means of engagement to motivate and connect all young children with the classroom learning content. An engaged child is more likely to become an expert learner.

I recently had the opportunity to be a panelist for a webinar about preparing teachers to use the UDL framework in early childhood settings. Dr. Eva Horn was one of my co-panelists, and she talked a lot about the importance of creating a classroom environment that leads to joyful learning. This is exactly what happens when we focus on offering multiple means of engagement in our classrooms. When we engage and motivate learners, we add joy to their learning experience and, as a result, we add joy to our own teaching experience.

ENGAGING CHILDREN

Basically, the principle of multiple means of engagement encompasses the ways we keep learners interested in classroom instruction. This principle answers the following questions: What do we do to help children get excited about learning? What do we do to keep them excited? What do we do when children are not excited? The principle of multiple means of engagement supports the affective brain network and answers the question "Why should I learn?" (Glass, Meyer, and Rose 2013). The affective network of the brain controls our emotions and how we process feelings and experiences (Kim et al. 2016). Research from the first two decades of the twenty-first century discusses how the UDL framework aligns with the ways our brain functions. Because I want our focus to be practical, I am not going to dive deeply into brain science here, but I recommend checking out the CAST website for a comprehensive explanation of the latest research supporting this approach.

As we think about the UDL principles, it is critical that we consider the first word of each principle: *multiple.* We do not use just one strategy to engage children. Instead, we use a variety of methods to help ensure that all children become engaged, excited, and motivated about being in our classrooms and learning developmentally appropriate content.

As I noted in the introduction, CAST (2018) has developed a set of checkpoints that align with each of the three UDL principles. The checkpoints offer us further clarification for using the principle to support children's learning. Three checkpoints align to each principle, to address the areas of accessing knowledge, building knowledge, and internalizing knowledge. Each includes suggestions for how to implement them. Figure 2.1 offers an overview of the three checkpoints for the principle of multiple means of engagement.

Because UDL is based on flexibility and there is no specific way to use the UDL framework, there is no list of specific strategies that you must use when considering this principle in your classroom. As a teacher, you must decide what is right for you and for your setting. However, there are some commonly used strategies for increasing motivation and engagement of young children that are supported by research. In the rest of the chapter, I discuss some of these

Figure 2.1

CAST's UDL Checkpoints for Multiple Means of Engagement

UDL Checkpoint	Aligned Strategies Discussed in this Chapter
Checkpoint 7 (Accessing Knowledge): Provide options for recruiting interest.	• Providing choice • Using classroom materials aligned with children's individual interests and cultures • Including hands-on learning activities
Checkpoint 8 (Building Knowledge): Provide options for sustaining effort and persistence.	• Providing choice • Offering opportunities to learn with others • Including hands-on learning activities
Checkpoint 9 (Internalizing Knowledge): Provide options for self-regulation.	• Teaching self-monitoring and self-evaluation

Figure adapted from CAST 2018.

strategies: providing choice, using classroom materials aligned with children's individual interests and cultures, offering opportunities to learn with others, hands-on learning activities, and self-monitoring and self-evaluation. Keep in mind, though, that these are just a few ways that you can increase engagement for the children in your classroom—there are countless additional ways to motivate young learners!

PROVIDING CHOICE

I love having choices throughout my day. Just today, as I am writing this book, I have made numerous choices about what will make writing joyful (even though it is so hard and can be very discouraging). I have chosen to sit by a blazing fire with a mug of coffee, fuzzy socks, and my laptop on my lap. On other days, I choose to work from my desk with an iced coffee, a notepad and a pink pen, and classical music playing in the background. And yet on other days, I pack up my laptop and head to my favorite local coffee shop for a latte, no Wi-Fi to distract me, and the sounds of others working at tables around me. As an "expert learner" who aims to become an expert writer, I make the choices that lead to my success in daily writing tasks. Those choices may change from day to day to accommodate my needs and the tasks I must complete that day. I suspect that you do the same as you write lesson plans, respond to parent emails, fill out paperwork for your preschool director or principal, and complete other critical teacher tasks. Take a moment to close your eyes and think about the choices you have made today to lead to your success. Consider how the tasks may have been less joyful or harder if you had made different choices. In addition, consider how the choices you make have changed over time as you have learned more about your preferences as a learner and a person.

Just like us adults, children like to make choices, and having the chance to make choices can increase their engagement in tasks and make learning more joyful for them. Providing choice not only increases engagement in learning but also helps address equity issues. A research study funded by the Lego Foundation found that when young children are provided the opportunity to engage in free and guided play that offers choice, teachers are better able to close achievement gaps and address equity issues (Dowd and Thomsen 2021). Additional research has found that choice increases motivation, supports emotional regulation skills, increases communication skills, and can decrease challenging behaviors in young children (Elliott and Dillenburger 2016; Roche 2018; Jolivette et al. 2004; Green, Mays, and Jolivette 2020).

Providing more choices yet ensuring children meet expected learning outcomes can be challenging. To help me as I consider this, I have created a list of questions that I ask myself. Take the following scenario:

We are exploring water buoyancy through a science activity. The children must understand the idea that some things will sink and others will float. At this time, I do not need all of them to understand why this occurs but simply to know that it does occur. In the past, I have taught this lesson during circle time by putting objects into a clear bucket filled with water. Typically, I used about a dozen items for this demonstration, and about half of the items sank, while half floated. As I put each item into the bucket, I would ask the children what happened. After circle time, children rotated through centers; in the science center, they explored this concept using the same clear bucket of water with a different group of items. Each child received a clipboard with their Science Recording Log that showed a photo of each of the items for testing. Children would draw a picture next to each item to indicate whether it sank or floated.

There are some things I cannot or will not adapt as I change this lesson. We must use water and a variety of classroom items, and I still will require children to log what they see, but I am willing to provide choices for how they log it. As I think about ways I can add choice to this lesson, I have a few ideas. First, I could provide more items to test and let the children select which ones to use. The challenges I see with that is my Science Recording Log would either need to include photos of every possible item and they would leave some blank, or the log would include no photos and the children would need to draw their own. In addition, it is possible that they would select only items that float (or sink) and then would end up not understanding the concept. I could provide choice in how they complete the Science Recording Log: I could offer the paper on a clipboard as I have always done and also offer a simple document they could complete on the class iPads. This will mean a bit more initial prep time for me as I create the form on the iPad, and I might need to monitor the children a bit more closely in the science center to ensure they are not doing anything else or getting water on the iPads. I could also let them choose who is in their group for centers that day, but the last time I did that with this class, one child ended up in tears because nobody wanted to be in her group (we ended up having a great impromptu lesson on caring for others that day but had to save the planned centers for the next day). Considering these options, I am going to offer the two different ways to complete the Science Recording Log. A lot of the children love using technology, so that option may be very motivating for some of them, and this choice will not affect their ability to learn the concept of buoyancy.

Figure 2.2

Decision Process for Providing Choice

1. What is the learning objective for this lesson or activity? What must the children learn?

2. How have I traditionally taught the activity?

3. What tools have I used to teach this lesson in the past that I consider nonnegotiables? What am I unwilling or unable to change in the way I teach this?

4. What aspects of the lesson/activity might lend themselves well to choices?

5. What choices am I willing to offer? What are the pros and cons of those choices?

6. Are the choices I am willing to offer truly choices that children would select?

www.redleafpress
.org/cyl/2-2.pdf

Figure 2.2 offers these questions for you in a list format so that you can use them as you consider how to offer choice in your own classroom.

I hope you noticed a few things as you read through the scenario and looked at the list of questions. As teacher, I want to motivate and engage learners, but I also must ensure that the learning objective is still met. I cannot select a choice that will prevent children from learning the required content. Second, when I consider choices to offer, I need to ensure that the choices I offer are things with which I am comfortable. I do not want to offer a choice that will irritate me. For example, I would never offer a choice of letting children scream out an answer because screaming bothers me, and there is a chance that I would make them stop doing it even if I offered it as a choice. I also need to ensure that the choices I offer are things that children might actually want to do. If I offer one option that is something children will do and another they won't, I am not really providing a choice. For example, if I gave the children in my classroom the choice of doing the science experiment either during centers time or during free-play time, for most children that would not really be a choice, as they are not going to give up their free-play time for work. Finally, you might notice that I considered only two options for each choice. For young children (as for older children and adults), too many choices can be overwhelming and prevent them from making a choice (Iyengar and Lepper 2000); this phenomenon is known as *overchoice* (Muench 2010). In addition, too many options can be overwhelming for you as a teacher. Keep it simple. Offer choices, but don't offer unlimited choices or unnecessary choices.

As you begin to think about ways to offer choices in your classroom, I want to offer you a few simple ways to do so. Nearly unlimited ways exist for offering choices in your preschool or kindergarten classroom, and this is just a short list to get your creative juices flowing. You can

- offer the choice of a crayon or a marker for coloring;

- allow children to sit or stand during circle time;

- offer the option to sit at the table or stand at an easel to do art projects;

- allow children to use technology for some tasks;

- offer a choice of foam or wooden blocks for building; or

- allow children to work on a task alone or with a partner.

As you consider the use of choice in your classroom instruction, it is also vital that you think about the relevance of this practice (or any practice suggested in this book) within your school's learning philosophy. In chapter 5 of this book, I talk a bit about using UDL within a variety of teaching philosophies. For now I want to address the concept of choice within Reggio Emilia–inspired classrooms. Because child-led learning is the norm in these settings, young children are accustomed to making a variety of choices throughout the day. With this in mind, it may be appropriate to offer more than two or three options for children in these classrooms. Conversely, for children learning in more teacher-directed classrooms, choice is not the norm, and children will likely be more successful when offered only two options for each choice-based activity and explicitly taught how to make choices.

USING CLASSROOM MATERIALS ALIGNED WITH CHILDREN'S INDIVIDUAL INTERESTS AND CULTURES

A second strategy to engage young children is using classroom materials that are aligned with their interests (Lohmann, Hovey, and Gauvreau 2018) as well as their cultural backgrounds. When I talk to early childhood teachers, they often describe the interest-based learning units they include in their classrooms. Dinosaurs, fire trucks, and princesses seem to be popular themes in many classrooms. When we connect our learning content to children's interests, we can increase engagement, motivation, and joy in the learning.

I use many interest-based learning units in my classroom, but I distinctly remember doing a unit on rodeos during the Houston Rodeo one year. A few of the children in my classroom had attended the rodeo and wanted to talk nonstop about horses, cowboys, and bull riding. During outdoor time, every piece of playground equipment became a horse to ride, and the toys in the classroom transformed into cowboy clothes, trophies for good rides, and other rodeo paraphernalia. I decided to capitalize on this excitement by connecting many of our learning activities for the following few weeks to cowboys and horses. At the time, we were working on counting, patterns, and sorting in mathematics and on letter sounds and story sequencing in literacy. So we counted cowboy hats, sorted horses by color, made patterns using pictures of cowboy hats and spurs, and sequenced the events in stories about cowboys. The children in my classroom loved it, and using their current interests helped me ensure they all achieved the learning targets for that time period.

There are a variety of simple ways to incorporate interest-based learning into your own classroom without changing the learning goals for the lesson. Simple ideas for supporting numeracy include

- counting items related to the theme (counting dinosaur figurines);
- creating counting cards in shapes related to the theme (cutting out truck shapes and putting a number on some trucks and a quantity of stickers on other trucks; children then match the truck with a number on it to the truck that has the same number of stickers);
- making patterns using items related to images of children's interests (dog, cat, dog, cat); and
- sorting items (sorting images of princesses by their hair color).

You can also support children's literacy development while connecting to their interests:

- reading books to the class that align with interests (reading *The Snowy Day* to the class on the first snow of the year)
- having children act out stories related to their interests (acting out the scenes of *Where the Wild Things Are*)
- putting images of the events of a story into the correct order (printing photos of the foods the caterpillar eats in *The Very Hungry Caterpillar* and having children put the photos in the order in which the caterpillar eats the food)
- creating letter-matching cards in shapes related to the theme (cutting out dinosaur shapes and putting one uppercase or lowercase letter on each shape; children then match the dinosaurs with the same letter)
- sounding out words from stories aligned with the theme (sounding out the word *dog* when the teacher reads *Bark, George*)

In addition to engaging children by incorporating their interests into our instruction, we can also increase their motivation by being intentional in reflecting their culture in our instruction and our classroom materials (Ainley 2006). We must ensure that the toys in our classrooms come from a variety of cultures and are diverse; these classroom materials should reflect not only the cultures of the children in our classroom but also cultures that are not represented. As you consider ways to include diversity in your classroom, though, I caution you against falling into cultural stereotypes that do not accurately represent a culture or belief system.

Resources for Diversifying Classroom Materials

I recommend starting with these resources if you are seeking more in-depth and expert advice in diversifying the materials in your classroom.

Mirko Chardin and Katie Novak, *Equity by Design: Delivering on the Power and Promise of UDL* (Thousand Oaks, CA: Corwin Press, 2021).

Andratesha Fritzgerald, *Antiracism and Universal Design for Learning: Building Expressways to Success* (Wakefield, MA: CAST Professional Publishing, 2020).

Jennifer Katz, *Teaching to Diversity: The Three-Block Model of Universal Design for Learning* (Winnipeg: Portage and Main Press, 2012).

Angèle Sancho Passe, *Creating Diversity-Rich Environments for Young Children* (St. Paul, MN: Redleaf Press, 2020).

We also need to consider ways to include images of children and adults with disabilities in our classroom materials. A variety of toy manufacturers, such as Mattel's Barbies and American Girl dolls, are now making dolls that have disabilities or offering doll accessories such as hearing aids, prosthetic legs, wheelchairs, and walkers. Similarly, the Lego company sells Lego people with physical disabilities. Including toys such as these in your classroom can help children with disabilities feel more included in learning and help normalize physical differences for children without disabilities. This will in turn increase their engagement in the classroom.

Figure 2.3

Diversity in Media

Diverse Books

Abuelo by Arthur Dorros (main character is Latino)

Ada Twist, Scientist by Andrea Beaty (main character is African American)

Charlotte and the Quiet Place by Deborah Sosin (main character has autism)

The Deaf Musicians by Pete Seeger and Paul DuBois Jacobs (main characters are deaf)

Festival of Colors by Kabir Sehgal and Surishtha Sehgal (main characters are from India)

Goldy Luck and the Three Pandas by Natasha Yim (main character is Chinese)

King for a Day by Rukhsana Khan (includes a main character who uses a wheelchair)

Last Stop on Market Street by Matt de la Peña (main characters are African American; plot of book includes viewing cultural differences in neighborhoods)

Princess Hair by Sharee Miller (main characters are African American)

Under My Hijab by Hena Khan (main character is Muslim)

Welcoming Elijah: A Passover Tale with a Tail by Lesléa Newman (main characters are Jewish)

Diverse TV Shows

Alma's Way on PBS (main characters are Latino and one character has a physical disability)

Daniel Tiger's Neighborhood on PBS (one character has a prosthetic leg and one character is Black and autistic)

Goldie & Bear on Disney Jr. (one character uses a wheelchair)

The Magic School Bus Rides Again on Netflix (main characters are from a variety of cultural backgrounds)

Molly of Denali on PBS (main character is Native Alaskan)

Sesame Street on HBO and PBS (includes children from a variety of cultural backgrounds, celebrates holidays from various religions, and includes a child with autism)

The Snowy Day on Amazon Prime (main characters are an African American family)

Children love to read stories and do activities when they can personally connect with the characters through books and media that reflect the diversity in our classrooms and in our communities. In some cases, it is appropriate to support classroom instruction with movies and television shows that align with learning. When we use media, we need to ensure that our selections offer a diverse list of characters that reflect the diversity in our classrooms and communities. Figure 2.3 offers a list of books and movies that include diverse children and families that may align with learning in the preschool and kindergarten classroom; keep in mind that this list includes only a small portion of the materials you can select to include in your classroom.

OFFERING OPPORTUNITIES TO LEARN WITH OTHERS

Young children love to interact with other children. A recent study found that preschoolers sustain engagement in science and mathematics activities for longer when they engage in learning tasks with others versus when they work alone (Master, Cheryan, and Meltzoff 2017), and additional research indicates that collaborative learning leads to academic benefits (Bergman and Morphew 2014). Another study found that preschool and kindergarten children had more correct answers in problem-solving tasks when they worked with a partner than when they worked alone (Rittle-Johnson et al. 2013). Finally, research indicates that collaborative learning increases children's perceptions about their own competence in learning a specific subject or material (Altermatt et al. 2002).

Based on the research, it is clear that children benefit from learning in collaboration with their classmates. With this in mind, early childhood educators must be prepared to implement best practices in collaborative learning. Iliana Alanís (2018) reports that children get the most benefit from collaborative learning when they work in pairs, especially when that learning involves language development. This is because having two children in the group allows each child the maximum opportunity to engage in learning and interacting with a peer. That being said, some learning activities, such as science experiments that require many materials, lend themselves better to small groups, so don't shy away from putting young children in groups for learning activities. On some days or for certain activities, young children should have the opportunity to select their own pairs or groups. For other activities, the teacher should select the groups, such as when the activity has been differentiated to meet student needs and abilities. And, in some cases, it is appropriate to allow children the option of working alone, in a pair, or in a small group.

Teachers can use collaborative learning in countless ways to support student engagement. A few effective options are described in figure 2.4.

Figure 2.4

Ideas for Incorporating Collaborative Learning in the Early Childhood Classroom

Strategy	Description	Example
Think-Pair-Share	Children are placed in pairs, and each pair is given a problem to solve. Each child starts by individually thinking about the problem and potential solutions. Then the partners share their ideas with one another and work collaboratively to identify a potential solution.	Yasmin and Kaoru are working together in the science center. Mr. Ramirez has asked them to build a house for the Three Little Pigs. On their table, they have toothpicks, marshmallows, gumdrops, straws, and a small paper pig. Mr. Ramirez sets a timer and tells the children they must stay silent and think about how to build the house. After two minutes, the timer rings and the children begin sharing ideas. After listening to each other and refining their plan, they begin to build.
Learning Games	Children are placed in pairs or groups to play a commercially made or teacher-created game that will enhance their learning.	Amari, Hakim, and Xavier have chosen to work together during math centers time. Together, they play the collaborative games "Feed the Woozle" and "Count Your Chickens." Playing these games together leads the boys to laugh and smile as they work.
Round Robin	Children are placed in groups or work together as an entire class. Each child takes a turn answering the same question, and children encourage one another during the activity. There are several variations for this activity, including having young children draw pictures or act out their ideas.	Today Ms. Johnson's class is working on the sounds made by the letter *S*. During circle time, each child is asked to think of a word that begins with this sound and then act it out for the class. The rest of the children try to guess the word.

TEACHING SELF-MONITORING
AND SELF-EVALUATION

A fifth strategy for engaging young children in the classroom is teaching them to self-monitor and self-evaluate their own learning and behaviors (Lohmann, Hovey, and Gauvreau 2018). Earlier in the chapter, we discussed the strategy of providing young children with choices, which offer them the opportunity to have control over their own learning. Having children monitor their own learning and behavior is another way to give them control, which can enhance their engagement. The research indicates that, with guidance, all children can learn to self-monitor (Perels et al. 2009), and doing so can increase their self-determination skills. *Self-determination* describes the set of skills required to manage one's own needs and make appropriate decisions for achieving short-term and long-term goals (Deci and Ryan 2012). Ultimately, we want all children to have strong self-determination, and we can help them gain these skills while also increasing their learning engagement by including self-monitoring in our instruction. There are a variety of ways that we can do this, including class-wide monitoring systems, individual monitoring systems that are the same for each child, and individualized monitoring systems that are tailored to each learner. We can also use a combination of these three strategies.

A class-wide system that I recommend is group contingencies. Essentially, the entire class receives a reward when the class as a whole meets classroom expectations (Naylor, Kamps, and Wills 2018). The concept of group contingencies for supporting overall classroom behavior challenges is well supported in research (Helton and Alber-Morgan 2020; Naylor, Kamps, and Wills 2018; Pokorski 2019), and the use of this strategy has been shown to improve young children's engagement in learning (Pokorski 2019). This group dependence encourages children to support one another in meeting the class goals (Helton and Alber-Morgan 2020). I often see teachers use pom-poms in a jar or tally marks on the whiteboard to indicate that the class is meeting expectations. When a certain goal is reached (a jar full of pom-poms or one hundred tally marks), the class receives a reward, such as a candy party or extra playtime on the playground. While this system increases children's engagement in the classroom, we can further motivate learning by adding a self-monitoring component to this system.

Instead of the teacher determining when the class has met the expectation, the class members can make the determination. Consider this scenario:

Mr. Tesfaye's preschool class receives stickers on their class chart. When the chart is full, the class will receive a donut party. While Mr. Tesfaye feels that this reward system has had a positive impact on student behaviors, he wants to give the children more responsibility for managing themselves and their behaviors. To do this, he decides to adapt the reward system to include self-monitoring and evaluation. After each activity, the children who have the assigned class jobs of teacher's helper and secretary have a short discussion together to decide if the class should earn a sticker for their behavior during that activity. At first Mr. Tesfaye noticed that the children gave themselves a sticker after every activity. When he disagreed with their assessments, he asked them to explain why they believed they earned a sticker and re-minded them of behavior challenges that arose during the activity. Over time Mr. Tesfaye has noticed that the children are becoming more skilled at evaluating their behaviors.

If you consider using this system in your classroom, I do have a quick word of caution. If one (or two) children are often the reason the class does not get the reward, there may be social implications from classmates who are upset. If you have a child in the classroom who struggles to meet the expectations, you might consider making the criteria that 95 percent of the class must do as expected, to allow for one child to make mistakes without preventing the class from getting a reward. In addition, you must ensure that you provide individualized support to help the child succeed in the future.

In addition to class-wide self-monitoring, we can use this same strategy with individual children for both behaviors and learning. When we are providing instruction on a specific skill, we need to ensure that all learners understand the concept. Traditionally, we evaluate this through official methods, such as projects, tasks, and observations of young children. But these summative evaluations sometimes occur late in the learning process, and we can better support learners if we know earlier that they do not understand a concept. To address this, we can teach children to self-monitor their own learning and provide them ways to indicate to us when they need extra support during a classroom activity or at the end of a structured lesson. We teach children to self-monitor in the same ways that we teach every other skill—we talk about it, model it, practice as a group, offer opportunities for individual practice, provide frequent and specific feedback, and reteach as necessary. Figure 2.6 provides a few simple ways that children can show us they understand (or don't understand) a classroom concept. I suggest that you do your own evaluations of children's understanding in addition to their self-evaluation, as some children may feel uncomfortable admitting that they do not understand a concept or do not realize they are missing something important.

Figure 2.6

Self-Monitoring and Self-Evaluation Strategies

Thumbs-up or thumbs-down	Standing up or staying seated
Holding up red or green card	Pointing to smiley face or frowny face
Staying on the carpet after circle time or going to the table to start independent work	Circling the word *yes* or *no* on a piece of paper

Figure 2.7

Self-Monitoring of Behavior

Classroom Activity	Did I Meet Expectations?
Arrival/Table Work	👍 👎
Circle Time	👍 👎
Free Play	👍 👎
Centers	👍 👎
Snack	👍 👎
Playground	👍 👎
Centers	👍 👎
Group Time	👍 👎
Cleanup/Going Home	👍 👎

In addition to these class-wide strategies for self-monitoring learning, some young children benefit from individualized self-monitoring systems designed to support their specific needs. This can be especially beneficial for children with disabilities who need additional supports to be successful. These individualized self-monitoring systems can take many forms. Figure 2.7 offers an example of a self-monitoring system a young child might use to track their own behaviors during classroom activities. If the child is not yet a reader, I recommend using photographs or clip art images instead of the words in the left-hand column. To use this tool, the child could choose a variety of ways to indicate whether they met the expectations, including putting a sticker on the correct thumb in each row or highlighting or circling the thumbs-up or thumbs-down for each activity. Alternatively, leave the row below Did I Meet Expectations? blank and put a sticker or mark in the spot each time they meet expectations.

www.redleafpress
.org/cyl/2-7.pdf

In addition to assessing behavior, self-monitoring can also help children learn to regulate their own hygiene skills. Figure 2.8 shows a sample self-monitoring sheet for supporting a young child in using the restroom. Similarly to figure 2.7, you can leave the Completed? row blank and place a sticker when expectations are met.

www.redleafpress
.org/cyl/2-8.pdf

As you can see from these two examples, self-monitoring tools should be simple so that young children can complete them independently. These forms can be printed as onetime use papers that are thrown away after use, or they can be laminated and used over time. (But for hygiene purposes, if it includes the toilet, I suggest making them onetime use!)

Figure 2.8

Restroom Steps Self-Monitoring

Steps in Use of Restroom	Completed?	
Get to toilet on time	Yes	No
Lift toilet lid	Yes	No
Sit down	Yes	No
Use toilet	Yes	No
Wipe	Yes	No
Flush toilet	Yes	No
Close toilet lid	Yes	No
Wash hands	Yes	No
Throw away paper towel	Yes	No
Return to classroom	Yes	No

MOVING FORWARD

It is vital that teachers engage and motivate young learners. Through providing multiple means of engagement, you can accomplish this goal. In this chapter, we discussed five strategies for engaging children in the classroom:

- Providing choice
- Using classroom materials aligned with children's individual interests and cultures
- Offering opportunities to learn with others
- Including hands-on learning activities
- Teaching children self-monitoring and self-evaluation methods

While each of these strategies is effective and I recommend that you incorporate them into your classroom, remember that this is not a comprehensive list. You can motivate learning and encourage young children to become expert learners in countless ways. As you begin to implement this UDL principle, discover what motivates and excites the children in your classroom—what leads them to be joyful learners. Use this knowledge to further engage them.

As we conclude this chapter and move on to the next UDL principle, find something that motivates and engages *you* in learning. For me, it might be a set of felt-tip pens in a variety of colors and a new notebook so that I can take color-coded notes about what I am reading. Add some coffee and chocolate to that and I am a very excited learner! Once you find what will sustain your motivation, I will meet you in chapter 3 to talk about using multiple means of representation to support learning.

Multiple Means of Representation: Designing Instruction to Support the Unique Needs of All Children

Miss Franklin is excited for science in her kindergarten classroom this week. It is the beginning of spring, and she is teaching about the life cycle of plants. On the first day of the week, she introduces the concept by reading From Seed to Plant *by Gail Gibbons. Then she uses her interactive whiteboard to show a short video that illustrates the plant life cycle. Next she gives each child pictures of the stages of the life cycle and the children work in pairs to put them in the correct order. After this each child plants a bean seed in a paper cup. The children are given the option to use a spoon or their hands to put dirt in the cup. The cups are put on the windowsill so that the children can watch for the seeds to sprout. Miss Franklin ends the lesson by reading* The Tiny Seed *by Eric Carle. Each child has their own copy to follow along with her reading. As the week continues, Miss Franklin reads a variety of other books about the plant life cycle, and the children complete puzzles and play games that require them to put the stages of the plant life cycle in the correct order. By the end of the week, each child in Miss Franklin's classroom knows the life cycle of a plant. And they can hardly wait for the seeds to sprout!*

Like Miss Franklin, you likely look for many ways to help the young children in your classroom understand what you are teaching. You use a variety of tools and strategies to introduce the same information. When you do this, you are meeting the UDL principle of multiple means of representation. You are helping ensure that all learners in your classroom can access the information and will learn the content.

When many of us were children, a common belief in the field of education was that we needed to teach to children's learning styles. And recent research tells us that many teachers of young children still believe this myth (Nancekivell, Shah, and Gelman 2020). Over time we have found that the concept of learning styles offers an incomplete understanding of how people learn and that people have learning preferences but not learning styles (Scott 2010). We now know that we all have ways that we prefer to access learning content, but most of us can learn in a variety of ways. Moreover, when information is provided to us in multiple ways, we learn it better (Meyer, Rose, and Gordon 2014). As teachers of young children, we want to support the learning of all children, so it is best practice to teach content in a variety of ways. In this chapter, I present five ways that preschool and kindergarten teachers can provide multiple means of representation in their classrooms: using a variety of learning materials, using visual supports, connecting instruction to previous learning or experiences, integrating technology, and modeling/thinking out loud. Remember, though, that these examples are just a few of the ways you can do this.

In chapter 1, we covered the UDL checkpoints and the alignment of teaching tools with these checkpoints. For multiple means of representation, there are three checkpoints: (1) provide options for perception, (2) provide options for language and symbols, and (3) provide options for comprehension. Figure 3.1 shows how the strategies discussed in this chapter align with these three checkpoints.

Figure 3.1

CAST's UDL Checkpoints for Multiple Means of Representation

UDL Checkpoint	Aligned Strategies Discussed in this Chapter
Checkpoint 1 (Accessing Knowledge): Provide options for perception.	• Offering a variety of learning materials • Using visual supports • Integrating technology
Checkpoint 2 (Building Knowledge): Provide options for language and symbols.	• Offering a variety of learning materials • Using visual supports • Integrating technology • Modeling and thinking aloud
Checkpoint 3 (Internalizing Knowledge): Provide options for comprehension.	• Offering a variety of learning materials • Connecting instruction to previous learning or experiences • Integrating technology • Modeling and thinking aloud

Figure adapted from CAST 2018.

OFFERING A VARIETY OF LEARNING MATERIALS

The first strategy for providing multiple means of representation in the early childhood classroom is to include a variety of materials in your instruction. If we look back at the vignette at the beginning of this chapter, we can see that Miss Franklin uses storytelling and hands-on activities to help the children in her classroom understand the stages of the plant life cycle. She also selects learning materials that connect to various senses. By reading to the children and showing them the pictures, Miss Franklin engages both visual and auditory learning. During the final story, when children hold copies of the book while she reads, Miss Franklin is also engaging their kinesthetic learning systems. Additionally, offering each child a copy of the book helps keep children with attention challenges more engaged in the story as they follow along, and it provides support to young children who have visual impairments and struggle to see the book when she holds it up while reading. By showing a video, the teacher further incorporates auditory and visual learning. She adds hands-on learning when the children put the images into the correct order while playing the games and doing the puzzles and when they plant the seeds.

As you reflect on ways to implement a variety of learning materials in your classroom, think about upcoming lessons you will teach and consider the materials you already use and how you use them. Ask yourself if you could use those same materials in a different way, perhaps thinking about how you have seen other teachers use the materials. Consider what challenges the children might face in using the materials in a new way. Then think about whether you have easy access to new materials that are developmentally appropriate for the children in your classroom, and brainstorm ways you could vary the materials you use to teach a concept.

Sometimes I see early childhood educators use a variety of learning materials, but they use those same materials in the exact same ways every single day. For example, they may read books, use puppets, and sing songs to talk about the weather, days of the week, and seasons during circle time. But then they don't include those materials in any other part of the school day. Books can support science instruction, math skills such as counting, social studies concepts, and so much more. Likewise, songs and puppets support learning in all subjects.

I like to walk around the classroom and look at the centers, especially the free-play centers. Countless toys can offer multiple means of representation and support children's engagement. Blocks are a fantastic tool for teaching mathematics skills such as counting, sorting, and patterns. Most classrooms include more than one type of blocks, so I recommend varying which ones you use. For example, on Monday, use the wooden blocks for hands-on mathematics instruction, use Lego bricks on Tuesday, foam blocks on Wednesday, cardboard blocks on Thursday, and homemade milk carton blocks on Friday. Use playground balls to teach about the physics concept of rolling motion, and test buoyancy with the toy trucks and sandbox toys. Similarly, consider using the food in the play kitchen for sorting purposes, and bring over dolls and stuffed animals to supplement puppets when acting out stories. When we think about using a variety of materials in our classrooms, we often don't need to purchase more tools. We just need to get creative and repurpose things we already have (or borrow things from the teacher next door).

USING VISUAL SUPPORTS

Visual supports are simply photographs or clip art that provide children with cues about expectations. Educators often use these tools to target the specific needs of children with disabilities such as autism (Meadan et al. 2011) as well as dual-language learners (Espinosa 2013). For these children, visual supports can remove language-based barriers to their learning. But these supports also enhance all young children's learning, especially when paired with oral language (Gauvreau, Lohmann, and Hovey 2019). They can improve academic learning and young children's interactions with peers, enhance play skills, teach routines and classroom expectations, and reduce challenging behaviors (Elimelech and Aram 2019; Ganz and Flores 2010; Gauvreau 2019; Gauvreau, Lohmann, and Hovey 2019; Gauvreau and Schwartz 2013). For young children, each of these areas is a vital part of the learning and development that occurs in the school setting.

You can use visual supports for instruction in many ways, and you are likely already using some of the following strategies. The important thing for using visual supports in the UDL framework is ensuring that the visuals are aligned with the oral language you are using, can be understood by young children, and are not too overwhelming, thus preventing young children from focusing on the message of the lesson. Focus on choosing images that are functional, not fancy; photographs, clip art, or drawings all work.

Visual supports can enhance young children's learning for virtually any academic skills taught in a preschool or kindergarten classroom, in both formal lessons and in informal interactions with young children. Figure 3.2 offers a few ideas for using visual supports to teach early numeracy skills. Similar tools can be used to add visual supports in other subject areas too.

Figure 3.2

Examples of Visual Supports for Early Numeracy Instruction

Examples of Supports	Scenarios Showing Their Use
Posters with numerals and the corresponding number of items	Mr. Finnegan asks the children in his preschool classroom to find the poster that includes a picture of five monkeys. He counts "one, two, three, four, five" as the children are looking for the correct poster on the wall. When they find it, Mr. Finnegan says, "Great job! Let's count the monkeys together. There are one, two, three, four, five monkeys on this poster."
Number line/hundreds chart	The children in Ms. Ramos's kindergarten class are learning to count and recognize numbers to one hundred. In the math center, Ms. Ramos has created an activity that asks children to listen to an audio recording of her counting to one hundred. The children are expected to follow along on a hundreds chart while they listen and point to the number as they hear it.
Felt cutouts of shapes	Mr. Li has been teaching his prekindergarten class about shapes. They have learned about circles, squares, triangles, and pentagons. Today, he is introducing them to hexagons. He explains to the class that a hexagon has six sides. Then he shows them a piece of felt that has been cut out into the shape of a hexagon. As a class, they count the sides, "one, two, three, four, five, six."
Dollars and coins	Rafael and Maria are playing in the home center. Maria is pretending to be a plumber who has just repaired the sink in Rafael's kitchen. She tells Rafael that he owes her "seven dollar cents." Mrs. Lopez overhears the conversation and goes over to talk to the children. She asks Maria if she wants Rafael to pay dollars or cents for her work. Then Mrs. Lopez opens up her wallet and shows the children what both a dollar bill and a penny look like. Maria decides that she would like dollars and says to Rafael, "Pay me seven dollars, please. Don't forget, those are the paper ones."

Visual supports can also increase young children's social interaction and play skills. As a teacher, I used many visual supports to aid the children in my classroom in making friends and interacting with their classmates. For example, one year a child in my classroom had limited verbal skills. He wanted to play with his classmates on the playground, but he did not know how to initiate play. Because his speech was hard to comprehend, his classmates did not know what he was saying when he asked them to play. He quickly learned that the fastest way to get a response from classmates was to hit them. Obviously, that was not a social interaction I wanted to continue, so I had to come up with an alternative. I created a simple visual support he could use to ask his classmates to play with him. On a three-by-five-inch note card, I put the words "Will you play with me?" and a clip-art image of two children playing on the swings together. I made several copies of the card and laminated them. Then I taught him how to use the card by pairing it with the spoken words "Will you play with me?" He quickly learned to use these visual tools to initiate play, and his classmates soon began to understand his speech patterns.

Some young children need frequent reminders about how to interact with peers and may use a variety of supports for different types of social interactions. A simple visual support with photographs or images of the steps in the interaction may help these children be successful. Engaging in an appropriate two-way conversation is challenging for many young children, but the use of a visual support can help. As the teacher explicitly teaches the steps of conversations, they can show each corresponding image. Then the child keeps their own copy of the steps to use when talking to classmates. The steps include (1) approaching a classmate, (2) looking the classmate in the eyes, (3) saying hello, (4) waiting for the classmate to say hello, (5) asking a question or making a short statement to the classmate, (6) waiting for the classmate to respond and listening while they speak, and (7) saying goodbye at the end of the conversation. Figure 3.3 offers an example of a very basic visual support for this purpose. Notice that the images are not fancy, and this visual support can be easily made on your computer using tools such as Microsoft Word or Google Docs. You don't need special applications or computer programs to create visual supports.

www.redleafpress
org/cyl/3-3.pdf

Figure 3.3

Visual Support for a Conversation

1. Walk up to your classmate.	
2. Look in their eyes.	
3. Say hello.	
4. Wait for your classmate to say hello.	
5. Make a short statement.	
6. Listen to your classmate's response.	
7. Say goodbye.	

Visual supports also make teaching classroom expectations and routines go more smoothly. All teachers have rules and routines they use in their classrooms. These differ for every teacher and are often very different from children's expectations in their homes. Some children easily learn new routines and expectations, but others need frequent reminders and supports to be successful. Although not all children in the classroom need these supports to be successful, they all can benefit from them as a reminder of what you would like them to do. I always suggest that every classroom have a posted list of the overarching classroom expectations, which some people refer to as rules. This poster should include three to five positively stated expectations, which are explicitly taught to the entire class and retaught frequently (Lohmann 2021).

Visual supports can be used to help children succeed in all daily routines and can take the form of simple images, checklists, or task analyses. As you think about creating these routine-based supports, ensure that they are developmentally appropriate. For example, for younger children, you may want to include only four or five steps. But kindergarten children who have already learned how to follow visual supports in their routines may be able to follow a dozen or more steps. Figure 3.4 provides suggestions for using visual supports with common routines in the preschool and kindergarten classroom.

Figure 3.4

Visual Supports for Routines

Arrival at School

- Photograph of each child inside their cubby

- Checklist with photographs of each step of the arrival procedure (take off backpack, hang backpack in cubby, take off coat, hang coat in cubby, take lunchbox and water bottle out of backpack, zip up backpack, put lunchbox and water bottle in lunchtime bin, go to table, begin independent table work)

- Photographs of the options for independent table work (puzzle, book, game, art project); I recommend keeping the options the same for at least one week, having a routine for each day of the week, or seeking other efficiencies here so that you don't need to re-create this visual support every day.

Circle Time

- Photograph of each child taped onto their carpet spot

- Visual schedule that shows the order of activities for circle time (sit on spots; sing "Hello Song"; listen to the teacher read a story; review the weather chart, calendar, phonogram of the week, and daily number; and sing songs)

- Visual supports that align with stories and songs (for "Old McDonald," you might use photographs of each animal and hold up the photograph while you sing about that animal)

- Images that remind children of expectations during circle time (such as a photograph of an ear to remind children to listen while others are speaking; this can be held up when the reminder is needed so that the teacher does not need to interrupt whoever is speaking to provide the reminder)

Centers

- Pictures (or the item itself) to label containers (a photograph of blocks attached to the blocks container)

- "My turn" cards that children can hold when it is their turn during a game or group activity

- Images of the steps to complete the tasks in the center (for the book listening center, the images could include sitting in the chair, putting on headphones, pushing START to begin the story, listening quietly, taking off the headphones when the story ends, and drawing a picture of their favorite part of the story)

Restroom

- Picture of the toilet being flushed posted in each stall to remind children to flush the toilet

- Task analysis posted next to the sink that shows steps for handwashing (turn on hot and cold water, place hands under water, put soap on hands, rub hands together while singing "Happy Birthday," put hands under water, get paper towel, dry hands, use paper towel to turn off water, throw away paper towel)

Snack

- Photograph of each child taped onto the table at their spot

- Checklist for cleaning up after snacktime

- Visual images of expectations (talk only when there is no food in your mouth, stay in your seat, raise your hand to get teacher help for opening snack containers)

Dismissal

- Checklist with photographs of each step of the dismissal procedure (get lunch box and water bottle from lunchtime bin, unzip backpack, put lunch box and water bottle in backpack, zip up backpack, put on coat, zip up coat, put on backpack, stand by cubby until everyone is ready)

- Images of school exit options to indicate where children should wait at dismissal time (taking the school bus, getting picked up in a car, walking with an adult, going to afterschool care)

In addition, visual supports can be used to reduce challenging behaviors in young children. We previously looked at using visual supports to remind young children of the classroom expectations, which can reduce challenging behaviors among all children. In addition, some children will benefit from more specific visual supports. One that I used frequently in my own classroom was a STOP sign. When children were exhibiting unwanted behaviors, I could simply hold up the sign. Other situations that lend themselves well to basic visual supports include the following:

- keeping your hands to yourself
- sitting in a chair
- using your listening ears
- following steps for turn-taking or sharing
- responding to frustration and conflict appropriately

By providing a variety of visual supports in your classroom and pairing them with verbal instructions as appropriate, you can support the learning and growth of the children in your classroom in a variety of developmental domains.

Visual Supports and Verbal Instructions

As we consider using visual supports in the classroom, remember that they should be paired with verbal instructions, especially as we are first teaching children how to use these tools. Doing so ensures that we are providing input in various ways for all learners and offering supports to meet the needs of children who have vision problems.

CONNECTING INSTRUCTION TO
PREVIOUS LEARNING OR EXPERIENCES

In chapter 2, we talked about using children's interests and cultural experiences to enhance their engagement in and motivation for learning. We can use these same concepts to provide multiple means of representation. Every child enters our classroom with a variety of experiences and previous knowledge that influences how they perceive and understand new information (Marzano 2004). When we connect new learning to previous knowledge, we help them understand the information in new ways while increasing the information's relevance to their lives. In chapter 2, I wrote about how I added horses and cowboys to my learning materials after the children in my classroom attended the rodeo. This is one simple way to connect learning experiences. Consider the following scenarios in which early childhood teachers use this strategy to support the learning of young children.

> *Mr. Pak is teaching a unit on the life cycle of a butterfly. The class has already talked about plant life cycles, and so the students are already familiar with the concept. Mr. Pak begins the lesson by asking the children to tell him what they know. The class tells him that plants start as seeds, then growth happens, and finally death. Mr. Pak tells the children that they are correct—just like plants, insects and animals have life cycles that begin with birth and end with death. He also reminds the children that plants can be small or large and can be a variety of colors, shapes, and textures. But regardless of those characteristics, all plants go through the same life cycle steps. Similarly, not all butterflies look the same, but they all have the same life cycle.*

In this scenario, we see how Mr. Pak uses previously introduced components of the same learning unit to help young children make connections between species. Preschool and kindergarten teachers can also help children make connections between learning in other subject areas or earlier classroom learning units, as illustrated in the story of Ms. Silva:

> *Ms. Silva is teaching about categorizing items as living or nonliving based on their characteristics. She begins the lesson by asking the children to think about what they have learned in mathematics. Last month they practiced sorting objects by shape and color. She asks the children how they knew which pile to put each object into. She then tells them that they will use similar skills to sort objects into groups based on the categories of living and nonliving.*

Additionally, teachers can help individual children in the classroom connect new information to experiences in their personal lives. These connections will be different for every child, as illustrated in the example of Mr. Johnson:

> *Mr. Johnson's kindergarten class is studying habitats. This week they are talking about the forest. Mr. Johnson knows that Asa's family has a cabin in the woods and goes there most weekends, so he asks Asa to share with the class what the outdoors looks like near the cabin. Mr. Johnson also knows that Talia watched a documentary over the weekend about black bears, so he asks her to tell the class what she learned from the show. Finally, Mr. Johnson knows that several of the children in the classroom enjoy the books* The Wild Woods *by Simon James and* A House in the Woods *by Inga Moore. He asks the children about the pictures in those books. After the children share that forests have lots of trees, can be dark, and include animals such as bears, deer, rabbits, and wolves, Mr. Johnson continues by teaching the children more about the forest habitat and the animals that live there. He concludes the lesson by talking about*

*the importance of protecting that habitat and asks the class
how they can personally do things to protect the trees and the
animals in the forest. Asa is especially concerned about making
sure the deer family that is often outside her window always has
a place to live.*

By connecting current learning goals to young children's previous experiences and background knowledge, teachers can enhance learning and provide multiple means of representation in the preschool and kindergarten classroom.

INTEGRATING TECHNOLOGY

In today's classroom, technology is a vital part of teaching and learning. Young children must be exposed to a variety of technologies and explicitly taught how to use those technology tools in a safe and responsible manner. When teachers use technology to support learning, they offer multiple means of representation. I do caution, though, that we need to use technology intentionally and never use it simply for the sake of using it. Using technology (or any teaching tool) should enhance children's learning. Technology use should not replace traditional hands-on learning for young children, such as blocks and art supplies (NAEYC and the Fred Rogers Center 2012). Technology tools should be only one aspect of instruction in a particular topic, as direct instruction and interaction from the teacher is still a vital component of all learning for young children.

Technology tools can be used for the entire class, or they can be provided for individual student learning during centers or independent work time. Figure 3.5 provides ideas for technology tools that can be incorporated into early childhood classrooms.

Figure 3.5

Technology Tools in Early Childhood Classrooms

Circle Time

- Audio recordings of songs that children can sing along to
- Weather applications on a tablet when discussing the weather
- Images aligned with a story or a song displayed on an interactive whiteboard
- Digital timers for games

Literacy Instruction

- Websites, such as Storyline Online, where children can listen to books being read aloud
- Tablet applications, such as Logic of English, for practicing phonograms
- Audio recordings of letter sounds
- Pen readers, which can read text from books to children
- Books on tape
- Word processing software for learning spelling words
- Reading applications on tablets
- E-readers with decodable books for children who are independent readers

Mathematics/Numeracy Instruction

- Talking calculators
- Websites and tablet applications for practicing mathematics skills, such as counting and basic addition and subtraction
- Computer games or activities created or purchased by you for sorting items or creating patterns
- Audio recordings of the teacher counting to one hundred
- Videos of objects being counted

Science

- Tablet-based digital observation logs for children to note what they observe in science experiments
- Digital cameras or tablets for children to take photographs of science experiments
- Computer-based drawing applications for children to create images of what they observe during science experiments
- Videos
- Tablet applications, such as Max & Ruby science educational games

As you consider how to use technology in your classroom, think of ways young children can assist you in building technology tools for their own learning. For example, audio recordings of information can help children gain extra practice and support in learning a concept, such as rote counting to one hundred. Consider having the entire class count to one hundred together, with you guiding them, recording them as they count. Then, place that recording in the listening center and have children whisper count along with the recording for independent practice.

MODELING AND THINKING ALOUD

Modeling and thinking aloud are other options for providing multiple means of representation in your classroom. Modeling is the act of showing children how to complete a task. We know that observation is an effective way to learn and that young children often want to emulate what they see the adults around them doing. When we create lesson plans, modeling is often used in the "I do" portion of the lesson. Modeling works for both academic and social skills; the teacher can complete the task personally or use puppets or other materials to demonstrate. Research indicates that we can improve the effectiveness of modeling when we tell children before we begin what they should watch for and then review what they saw after we are done (Andrieux and Proteau 2016). Figure 3.6 offers a few examples of how modeling might be used in the early childhood classroom.

I Do, We Do, You Do

One common way to write lesson plans is using the "I do, we do, you do" format. In the "I do" portion of the lesson, the teacher demonstrates how to complete the task. In the "We do" portion, the class works on the skill together. Finally, each child practices on their own and receives teacher feedback during the "You do" portion of the lesson.

Figure 3.6

Modeling in Early Childhood Classrooms

Literacy
- Modeling for children how to hold a book, turn the pages, and read each word on the page individually
- Demonstrating how to sound out words by looking at each phonogram individually
- Showing children how to orally sound out words to spell them
- Reading an adult book yourself during quiet times in the classroom so children can see that reading is a skill for all ages
- Demonstrating how to select a book in the library, based on both interest and reading skills

Mathematics
- Pointing to objects and counting them one by one out loud
- Demonstrating for children how to sort objects into groups by common characteristics
- Doing addition problems on the whiteboard while children watch
- Using money to purchase items in the classroom store

Social Skills
- Saying "please" and "thank you" to children, modeling how to request something from others
- Demonstrating for children how to take turns during a board game
- Showing children how to share their toys with one another

Personal Care
- Demonstrating for children how to wash their hands
- Using a tissue to blow your own nose, throwing away the tissue, and washing your hands

Video modeling incorporates technology into this strategy (Green et al. 2017). A video model is simply a recording of someone completing an action. The person in the video can be someone the children know, like a teacher or classmate, or a stranger. However, children's engagement and interest in watching the video may be enhanced when the video includes a familiar person and location. For example, if the children in my classroom frequently forget the process for cleaning up the table after snacktime (throw away the trash, push in the chairs, wipe down the table, check the floor for trash), I might create a video model showing me doing each of these steps. As I complete the steps, I state what I am doing so the children receive both oral and visual information about the expectations. I show the video at the end of snacktime each day to remind children what to do. As soon as the video ends, they are expected to clean up. If they miss a step, I can show them the video again. The video model allows children to view the same information as many times as they need to be successful.

Video modeling can be a useful tool in centers that require specific information. At each center, the teacher can record a short video model on a tablet. When children arrive at a center, they watch the video for instructions. If they forget expectations, they can easily watch the video more than once. Using video modeling at centers allows children to be more independent in completing tasks and provides teachers more time to focus on providing individualized supports for the students who need them.

Similar to modeling is the concept of thinking aloud, which is the process of orally explaining to children your thought process as you work through an activity. Thinking aloud can be especially beneficial for listening comprehension and mathematical skills as children hear how an adult mentally goes through the process of understanding the concept. It can be helpful to plan what you will say during a think-aloud and leave notes for yourself in the book or with your instructional materials so that you will remember what to say (Van Kleeck 2008). To better understand the thinking aloud strategy, consider the scenario of Miss Hassan.

Miss Hassan is currently focusing on increasing the listening comprehension of the children in her classroom. One way she does this is by thinking aloud when she reads a story aloud during circle time. Today she is reading the book Those Darn Squirrels and The Cat Next Door *by Adam Rubin. Before beginning to read, she shows the children the front of the book and tells them that the squirrels look familiar, like the squirrels from the book* Those Darn Squirrels!, *the first in the series, which they read the week before. This statement helps children see how to connect new information with previous knowledge. She then says, "Hmmm . . . in the other book, the squirrels cause a lot of trouble! I wonder if they will cause trouble in this book too! I really hope so because the squirrels were funny!" This statement demonstrates how to use previous knowledge and current information to make predictions. Miss Hassan then says, "Okay, class. I am ready to read this book. I am so excited and can't wait to find out what happens. Here is the first page. It looks like Old Man Fookwire is taking a nap. I wonder why he is doing that? What do you think? Also, I wonder why the title of the book mentions both squirrels and cats, but I don't see either one of them here. Maybe Old Man Fookwire is napping because he had a big lunch. Sometimes, when I have a big lunch, like on Thanksgiving, I get really tired and need a nap after lunch. I usually try to go to my bed to nap, but sometimes I am just so tired that I nap in a chair like he is doing. Maybe the squirrels and the cat will appear on the next page. There are a lot of pages left in the book. Also, I see that there is snow outside the window in this picture. I bet that means this story happens in the winter. I don't know where squirrels live in the winter—do they go south like birds do?"*

When Miss Hassan asks questions about what is happening and makes guesses about the book, she is demonstrating to the children in her classroom how to think about what they are reading and how to look at both the words and the pictures to better understand the story.

Through the use of modeling and thinking aloud, early childhood teachers can support preschool and kindergarten children in better understanding concepts being taught. When children have the opportunity to see others complete a task and hear an adult explain how they think through something, they are better able to complete the task themselves later on.

MOVING FORWARD

Over the past two chapters, we have discovered two of the three UDL principles and considered ways to use them in the preschool and kindergarten classroom to aid young children in becoming expert learners. In this chapter, we talked about how to meet the UDL principle of multiple means of representation through strategies such as providing a variety of learning materials, using visual supports, connecting instruction to previous learning or experiences, integrating technology, and modeling and thinking aloud. As you plan your classroom instruction this week, add one of these ideas to a lesson. If you are already doing most of these things, try something new or try doing something you already do in a new way. After you have tested it out, tweet at me to let me know how it is going! I can't wait to hear from you!

Multiple Means of Action and Expression: Creating Activities for Children to Show Their Expertise

Mr. Qiu and his preschool class have been learning about their city. They have visited important landmarks in their town, including City Hall, the park, the library, and the museum. They have learned the names of the main streets in their town and the basic history of their city. In addition, the children have learned about the important people in the history of their town, and last week they had a living wax museum, where they pretended to be people from their town's history. As they conclude the learning unit, Mr. Qiu wants to show various stakeholders the learning that occurred in his classroom. He wants parents, the school preschool director, and town officials who facilitated tours of landmarks all to see what the children have learned. In addition, he wants the final culminating project for the unit to reflect the interests of each child. He knows that this final project will take significant time to complete, so he wants to ensure that the children will stay motivated and engaged. With all of this in mind, he has decided to provide the children with choices for the final project. The children will work independently, but they can choose to use a tablet to create a video of what they have learned or use art materials to create a visual representation, which might include a poster with drawings or a model of the city built from recyclable materials or playdough.

Like Mr. Qiu, you use a variety of ways to allow the children in your classroom to demonstrate their knowledge. When you do this, you are meeting the third UDL principle, multiple means of action and expression, which is showcased in figure 4.1.

Figure 4.1

CAST's UDL Checkpoints for Multiple Means of Action and Expression

UDL Checkpoint	Aligned Strategies Discussed in This Chapter
Checkpoint 4 (Accessing Knowledge): Provide options for physical action.	• Integrating technology
Checkpoint 5 (Building Knowledge): Provide options for expression and communication.	• Offering language-based assessments • Conducting observations • Providing paper-based assessments • Integrating technology
Checkpoint 6 (Internalizing Knowledge): Provide options for executive functions.	• Teaching young children to set goals

In the early childhood classroom, we can offer multiple means of action and expression in many ways. In some cases, we want to offer children the choice of how to demonstrate their knowledge as Mr. Qiu did. When it is more appropriate or necessary to have all children complete the same activity, we can meet this UDL principle by ensuring that we use a different assessment for the next lesson. Think of it this way: your center director or school principal likely observes and evaluates you several times per year. That is one way your teaching effectiveness is evaluated. But, likely, parent feedback, student learning, and comments from other teachers are also considered. This offers a more comprehensive understanding of you as a teacher. And it ensures that if your principal observes only lessons that do not go well or days when there are behavior challenges in the classroom, they are still getting information from other sources that show your success. Similarly, when we use various assessment tools, we gain a better understanding of what the children in our classrooms know and can do.

It is important to assess the learning of all young children because it helps us to evaluate the knowledge and skills that children have mastered, identify their strengths, see the learning needs of individual children and the entire class, and monitor progress to see growth in learning (Wiggins and McTighe 2005). When we hear the term *assessment*, people often think we mean a test or an examination, but this is generally not the case. An assessment is simply a teaching tool that assists us in better understanding young children's learning. As teachers, we are constantly conducting assessments, even when we don't realize it. When we observe young children at play and think about their social-skill development, we are conducting an assessment. When we look at art projects and compare them to previous art, we are conducting an assessment and evaluating progress. When children complete a learning activity, we are conducting an assessment. Most assessments in an early childhood classroom are not for grades but rather are designed to help us improve our instruction to ensure that it best meets the needs of the learners in our classrooms.

In the preschool and kindergarten classroom, we can assess learning and offer multiple means of action and expression in many ways, including language-based assessments, observations, written activities, technology, and student goal setting. Some of these same strategies are also in the previous chapter concerning multiple means of representation. We can use these same tools, just in a different way, to evaluate young children's learning. In addition, you will notice that many of the examples presented in this chapter actually use a combination of assessment forms or tools.

OFFERING LANGUAGE-BASED ASSESSMENTS

There is a direct connection between verbal communication and early reading skills. Supporting young children in learning to communicate orally will benefit them as they later learn to read. Young children's verbal skills are still developing but give us some good information about their prereading skills. Children's communication skills also can be a good way to assess overall learning (Malec, Peterson, and Elsherief 2017). We can consider young children's learning with a focus on either their receptive or expressive language. *Receptive language* indicates that a child understands the words they hear, while *expressive language* means that a child can communicate their intended message through speech. When we use language-based assessments, we need to ensure that we are offering the appropriate modifications and supports within the assessment to meet the developmental needs of each child.

Assessments based on receptive language rely on children's listening comprehension skills. We can use these assessments in several ways; start by thinking about the scenarios in figure 4.2 and how you might do something similar in your own classroom. You will notice that the figure includes ideas for how to support children at different development levels within these assessments. Keep in mind that supports should be individualized to the strengths and needs of each child, so these are just a few ideas.

Figure 4.2

Ideas for Assessments Involving Receptive Language

Scenario	Information to Consider	Supports and Accommodations
Miss Mann has been teaching about the phonograms aligned with the letters *b*, *m*, and *t*. She wants to evaluate the extent to which the children in her classroom understand these sounds, so she has created a game in which she says a sound and the children run to find the corresponding letter (on a piece of paper) in the classroom and then bring it back to her. She has made sure that there are fifteen copies of each letter on the wall in her room so that each child will have their own copy.	Miss Mann must ensure that she is loud and clear when stating the phonograms so that children hear what she says. It is also important that the phonograms selected for this activity do not sound similar. For example, if Miss Mann had selected *m* and *n* for this activity, some children may be unable to distinguish between the two.	Miss Mann can repeat the phonogram as many times as needed to ensure the children hear it. Miss Mann can record herself saying the phonogram and let children who need additional support listen to the recording with headphones.

Scenario	Information to Consider	Supports and Accommodations
Mr. Bemba would like to assess the extent to which the children in his classroom recognize the numerals 1–20. He has provided each child with a worksheet that includes the numbers in random order, and he asks them to pull out their crayons for the task. He begins by saying, "Circle the number 7 with your blue crayon." Then he tells the children to circle the number 15 with the orange crayon. He continues until he has had the children circle each number.	Some children may not know how to circle the number, so be sure that you count it as correct if the child indicates the correct number with the correct color in any way.	Mr. Bemba can hold up images of the correct number of items when he orally states a number (a picture of five monkeys when he says five). Mr. Bemba can hold up the correct color crayon for each part of the activity to ensure that young children do not accidentally use the wrong color. Mr. Bemba can repeat the instructions for each number three to four times to give children time to process the information. Mr. Bemba can assess some children in a small-group setting instead of with the entire class so they can focus more easily and he can repeat as needed.
Mrs. Mumba needs to assess children's understanding of basic shapes, so she has created an activity for the listening center. At the listening center, there are glue, sheets of paper, and paper cutouts of various shapes, in addition to the tablets with headphones for children to listen to instructions. When the children start the recording, they hear instructions such as "Find the circle. Glue the circle at the top of your paper. Find the square. Glue the square under the circle. Find the triangle. Glue the triangle at the bottom of your paper."	Mrs. Mumba should include wait time in the recording to provide children time to complete the task of gluing shapes to the paper. Alternatively, she can have children pause the recording after each instruction. Young children need to understand directional information and know how to use the tablets to complete this task.	Mrs. Mumba can easily adapt the activity for the needs of various children, for example, by including fewer shapes or repeating the instructions. Mrs. Mumba can add to the recording using phrases such as "Find the triangle. The triangle has three sides. One, two, three," for children who need additional support.

In expressive language assessments, children orally tell us what they know. We must assess children either individually or in small groups so that we can hear each child's response. Figure 4.3 offers ideas for assessing the same skills from figure 4.2 but in a format that requires expressive language instead.

Figure 4.3

Ideas for Assessments Involving Expressive Language

Scenario	Information to Consider	Supports and Accommodations
Miss Mann is assessing phonogram knowledge in small groups at the teaching table. She holds up alphabet flash cards and asks the children to tell her the corresponding phonogram. As children answer, she listens closely and notes which children get the answer correct and which children need extra support in learning.	Children who are unsure of the answer may wait and listen for the other children in the group to respond. When this happens, Miss Mann should follow up with an individual assessment to get an accurate assessment of the child's knowledge.	Miss Mann can assess children individually as needed.
Mr. Bemba brings each child to his desk individually to assess their recognition of the numbers 1–20. He shows each child a number and asks them to state the number out loud. As the children respond, he notes their answers on his data collection form.	The numbers must be presented in random order so that children don't just count from one to twenty by rote. Some children will feel intimidated by knowing that classmates can hear them, so Mr. Bemba may consider conducting this assessment in the hallway or in a quiet space.	Mr. Bemba may assess some children on fewer numbers.
Mrs. Mumba wants to use technology to assess children's recognition of shapes. She has created an activity in the math center using the tablet. When the activity shows a shape, children record themselves saying the name of the shape. For example, Tara sees an image of a red circle and records herself saying "circle."	To be successful with this task, children must be comfortable using technology. If multiple children are completing the task at the same time, they may distract one another or copy one another's answers. To prevent this, I recommend putting the shapes in different orders within the activity on each tablet so that the children do not have identical assessments (but the activity still assesses the exact same skill).	Mrs. Mumba may sit with some children to support them in using the technology. Mrs. Mumba may offer a recording that children can listen to, which states the names of the shapes assessed. This will provide young children with options and help them remember how to say the names of the shapes.

CONDUCTING OBSERVATIONS

In its position statement on developmentally appropriate practice, the National Association for the Education of Young Children notes that accurately assessing young children's development can be challenging but that regular observations are one tool for better understanding their ongoing development. I recommend that early childhood teachers use observations to assess all skills but especially social-emotional skill development and personal care and behavior. Schools may purchase various assessment tools for evaluating these skills, but you can also create your own.

When you are assessing a skill that includes specific tasks or subskills, using an observation checklist can be a good way to track what you observe. Chapter 3 talks about using visual supports to help children remember the steps to washing their hands. In addition to teaching the children how to complete this skill and offering the visual supports, we also need to assess whether they can actually wash their hands or if they need extra support in learning some of the steps. Figure 4.4 is a checklist for assessing children's current skill level in hand-washing. You will notice that the left column is the list of tasks involved. The middle column asks the teacher to assess whether the child is currently able to complete the task or whether reteaching is required. The right column provides space for the teacher to write any additional relevant information. In this column, I might note that Johnny looks at the visual support to remember what comes next and that Ava does not remember the words to "Happy Birthday," so she does not know how long to rub her hands together.

Figure 4.4

Handwashing Task Analysis Checklist

Task	Level of Task Completion	Notes
Turn on the hot and cold water.	• Completed as expected • Needs some additional support in learning this task • Needs reteaching of this task	
Place your hands under the water.	• Completed as expected • Needs some additional support in learning this task • Needs reteaching of this task	
Put soap on your hands.	• Completed as expected • Needs some additional support in learning this task • Needs reteaching of this task	
Rub your hands together while singing "Happy Birthday."	• Completed as expected • Needs some additional support in learning this task • Needs reteaching of this task	
Put your hands under the water.	• Completed as expected • Needs some additional support in learning this task • Needs reteaching of this task	
Get a paper towel.	• Completed as expected • Needs some additional support in learning this task • Needs reteaching of this task	
Dry your hands.	• Completed as expected • Needs some additional support in learning this task • Needs reteaching of this task	
Use a paper towel to turn off the water.	• Completed as expected • Needs some additional support in learning this task • Needs reteaching of this task	
Throw paper towel away in the trash can.	• Completed as expected • Needs some additional support in learning this task • Needs reteaching of this task	

When you design a checklist to evaluate young children's mastery of a skill, be sure to track the explicit skills or steps in the process. To ensure that you are implementing an equitable assessment, your checklist should be used similarly for all learners and should be specific enough that any adult in the classroom could use it and get the same results you get. When collecting data, consistency is key, and we must ensure that we are tracking exactly what we observe, not what we think the child can do. If you consider figure 4.4, you will notice that each task is evaluated in one of three ways: completed as expected, needs some additional support in learning this task, or needs reteaching of this task. Before using this checklist, you must determine what qualifies to be listed in each category. For example, I might say that a child is marked as completed if they are able to get the paper towel with no help. Then I would say that one or two prompts (including looking at a visual support, verbal directions from an adult or peer, or physical assistance) qualifies as needing additional support. Finally, any child who required more than two prompts to complete a task would be marked as needing reteaching of that step. It is vital that you make the decisions about the number of prompts needed for each category before you begin assessing children. Be sure that you consider what is developmentally appropriate as you determine what qualifies.

While a checklist is ideal for evaluating some skills, other skills are best evaluated with an observation tracking sheet, which is more robust than a checklist. While the checklist provides you with a quick overview, an observation tracking sheet gives you specific details of what occurred. This tool can be used for academic, social-emotional, or behavioral observations. The key with creating these tracking sheets is to keep them simple and provide yourself plenty of space for taking notes. Observation tracking sheets can be paper-based, or you can use technology. Personally, I like to use Google Forms on my smartphone. I always have my phone in my pocket, so I can easily bring up the Google Form and fill it out, regardless of where I am. I have also seen teachers send themselves emails with observation information from their smartphones when they observe something they want to track. Figure 4.5 offers an example of a completed observation form that a teacher might use while observing a young child during arrival time. You will notice that this form is designed to track information over a period of time, but you can create the form to track only one occurrence if you prefer or if it better fits your situation. I do recommend, though, that you use a different form for each child or include a space for entering the student's name to keep the data more organized in the resulting spreadsheet populated by the form data.

Figure 4.5

Sample Observation Tracking Form for School Arrival

Date/Time/Location	Observation
February 21	Juan walked into the classroom and went to the block center and began to play. Mr. Bergen told him to put his coat away and follow the morning arrival routine. Juan went to his cubby and hung up his coat. Then he stood there until Mr. Bergen came over and pointed to the next step on the Arrival Task Analysis. Mr. Bergen pointed to each step before Juan completed it.
February 22	As Juan walked into the classroom, his mother told him to go to his cubby and follow the instructions for the morning routine. Juan went to his cubby and put away his coat and backpack. Then he went to the table and began doing a puzzle. Mr. Bergen came over and asked Juan if he had put his lunch box and water bottle away. When Juan said no, Mr. Bergen directed him to do so. Juan put them away and then returned to the table.
February 23	Juan went to his cubby and hung up his backpack. He began to walk away from his cubby until Suzie (the child whose cubby is next to his) reminded him of the other steps in the morning routine. Suzie stayed with Juan until he completed all of the tasks.

When you look at the observation tracking form, you likely notice the data that indicates that this student needs additional individualized support to be successful with the morning arrival routine. When we observe young children, we need to ensure that we are focused solely on the facts. We should record exactly what we see, without adding any opinion or personal interpretation. We also need to ensure that we are looking for the same information when we observe each child and are actively aware of any way that our personal biases may influence what we record. Consider this scenario:

> *Mr. Benedict wants to evaluate the problem-solving skills of the children in his classroom and is observing each child put together a puzzle. To get a better understanding of their skills, he is making a written observation record for each child. As he observes Kate, he records the following information:*

> *"Kate sat at the puzzle table at 9:31 a.m. She counted each of the twenty-five puzzle pieces while saying each number out loud and then said, 'Mr. Benedict, this puzzle has twenty-five pieces.' After counting the pieces, Kate put the pieces into two piles: those pieces that had a flat side and those that did not. She then looked at the art center, where Avni was playing, and yelled, 'Hey, Avni, guess what! This puzzle has twenty-five pieces, and I bet I can put it together in two minutes!' Then Kate looked back at the puzzle and began putting together the outside pieces. Once she had the frame together, she said 'Mr. Benedict—did you see that? I did it fast!' and then began putting together the inside portion of the puzzle. She completed the puzzle at 9:39 a.m. and yelled, 'Yay! Did y'all see that? I did that puzzle fast. It's a picture of three dogs, and I put it together quick!' She then took the puzzle apart and put it in the box."*
>
> *As he observes Kate, Mr. Benedict thinks that Kate is talking to those around her a lot and likely wants attention and acknowledgment for her work.*

Kate's social interactions and social-emotional needs were not the focus of this assessment, so Mr. Benedict did not record the information about Kate seeking the attention of others. Instead, he wrote down only exactly what he saw. This is an example of how observations should occur. We should be observing and recording only the information that is directly relevant to what we are assessing. If we observe something that we want to remember later, we can make a note elsewhere. I recommend that once you are done observing several children, you look over your observation notes to ensure that you recorded similar information for each child. Look specifically for any bias or personal opinions that might have affected your observations. Knowing your biases can help you directly prevent your interactions with and assessments of the children being influenced by them.

PROVIDING PAPER-BASED ASSESSMENTS

You can activate children's fine-motor skills through paper-based assessments. When we talk about using pencil and paper for assessments, many of us automatically think about traditional tests. While there may be some scenarios in which these traditional forms of assessment are appropriate for older children or adults, they are not a good solution for assessing the knowledge and skills of young children. However, there are several ways that we can use paper to assess young children's learning. We can provide multiple means of action and expression while doing so by varying the writing tools we offer children for completing their work on paper. Some ideas for paper-based assessments include the following:

- Write the answer (for example, the teacher says a phonogram and children write the corresponding letter on their paper).

- Color the answer (for example, color-by-number worksheets).

- Put a sticker on the answer (for example, children are provided with dot stickers that include a number written on each one. The paper includes objects to be counted, and children place the correct sticker on the group of objects).

- Use dot-making markers to stamp the answer (for example, children use markers to stamp all of the letter *Q*'s on the page).

- Glue the answers on the paper (for example, children are asked to glue images of living items on the left-hand side of the paper and images of non-living items on the right-hand side of the paper).

- Give children a stack of papers and ask them to put the papers in the correct order (for example, write the numbers 1–10 on note cards; children put the note cards in the correct order).

- Match papers (for example, children are provided papers that include uppercase and lowercase letters, and children match the letters).

- Draw a picture (for example, children draw a picture of their favorite part of a story).

- Paint a picture (for example, children paint a picture of the results of a science experiment).

Most young children can complete these types of options with little guidance or direction. None are time-consuming for a preschool or kindergarten teacher to create. Within the writing activity ideas, you can also switch up the medium and use crayons, markers, chalk, or pens. I also recommend that you let children select the writing tool they use to complete their work. Chapter 2 talks about providing choice to increase young children's engagement in learning. Letting children select their writing utensil is an easy way to provide choice.

Accommodations

While the majority of children can complete these paper-based assessments independently, some children may need accommodations. You may consider using a tablet-based drawing program instead of drawing or painting a picture or allowing children to work in pairs so that one child can verbally describe what should be written or drawn on the paper while the other child writes it.

Another way to adapt a paper-based assessment is to vary the type of paper: try copy paper, construction paper, card stock, poster board, note cards, sticky notes, paper grocery sacks, or cardboard boxes. When we think about paper-based assessments, there are so many ways to make the activity feel new and different for young children while still assessing their learning.

INTEGRATING TECHNOLOGY

Many of the same computer or tablet applications that young children use for learning also assess their progress. Because we know that technology is motivating for many young children (Couse and Chen 2010), using technology-based assessments can ensure that children demonstrate their true learning levels and do not lose motivation during the assessment. During the writing of this book, my son was in kindergarten and was working on learning his phonograms. Every day he used an application on my smartphone to practice, and I periodically looked at the data from the app to see his progress and better understand which phonograms were challenging for him. At one point, I noticed that he was making a mistake that many young children do by mixing up the sounds associated with the letters *b* and *d*. Having this information allowed me to specifically focus on these letters with him and evaluate this progress on learning the sounds by looking at the daily data from the app. Similarly, he learned to look at the data and figured out which sounds he had mastered and which ones he still needed to work on; he wanted to master everything, so he put extra focus on the phonograms that he was not getting correct. Technology tools that offer data and progress monitoring like this can be very valuable to teachers, especially as you aim to evaluate the learning of all young children in the preschool or kindergarten classroom. Figure 4.6 offers examples of other ways that preschool and kindergarten teachers can use technology to assess the learning of young children.

Figure 4.6

Scenarios of Technology Use for Assessing Learning

The children learned the life cycle of a pumpkin during October. Now Ms. Sang wants to know if the children in her class understand the stages of the life cycle. She creates a Google Slides presentation with	one stage of the life cycle on each slide. She puts the slides in random order. Each child is asked to rearrange the slides into the correct order.
Mr. Fatima's kindergarten class has been learning about their state, Colorado. They have studied the basic state history, learned that the capital is Denver, and discussed the state flower (the Rocky Mountain columbine) and the state bird (the lark bunting). Mr. Fatima needs to assess the information they have gained from this unit. Each child in the classroom uses the classroom tablet to make a	video recording of themselves discussing what they learned. After all the videos are recorded, Mr. Fatima watches them and learns that all of the children know the state capital, but some of them do not know any of the other information. He also finds that one child in his class can recall all the facts they learned in the unit.
Miss Daniels is preparing to assess the addition skills of the children in her classroom. She creates a Microsoft Word table for each student, with a	different addition problem in each cell. To answer the questions, children type in the answer to each mathematics problem.
Mrs. Ryan is assessing story comprehension skills and uses a web-based quiz program to better understand the comprehension levels of each child	in her classroom. To complete this assessment, the children watch a story being read and then answer questions about the story.

TEACHING YOUNG CHILDREN TO SET GOALS

A final suggestion for providing multiple means of action and expression is through teaching how to set goals. Learning to set goals is a vital component of success for learners of all ages (Philippakos 2020). When children engage in goal setting, they are more invested in their learning, and their executive functioning skills are enhanced. Executive functioning skills are those skills that support attention, focus, planning, and organization.

In the preschool and kindergarten classroom, we can support goal setting in many ways. We can set daily, weekly, monthly, or yearlong goals. We can even talk about our lifetime goals. We can help children set realistic goals and make a plan for achieving those goals. Figures 4.7 and 4.8 offer sample forms you can use to help children set their goals, but I encourage you to also consider ways to incorporate technology into goal development.

www.redleafpress
org/cyl/4-7.pdf

This weekly goal-setting form will likely require some support from the teacher to write the words and help the children identify action steps for achieving their goals. And, especially at first, young children may need support in identifying appropriate and achievable goals. Examples of goals that might be appropriate for a preschool or kindergarten child to achieve in one week include the following:

www.redleafpress
.org/cyl/4-8.pdf

- Throwing away their trash after lunch every day
- Learning to count to five
- Getting fifteen phonograms correct during the weekly assessment
- Getting all the +1 addition facts correct
- Saying "please" when requesting help from the teacher
- Giving one compliment to a classmate every day

Figure 4.7

Weekly Goals in Preschool

My name is _____.

This week, I want to _____

_____

_____.

If I want to achieve this goal, there are a few things I must do:

1. _____

_____.

2. _____

_____.

3. _____

_____.

Here is a picture of me achieving my goal.

Figure 4.8

Setting Adult Goals in Kindergarten

My name is _____.

When I grow up, I want to be a _____

_____

_____

_____

_____.

Here is a picture of me as an adult.

In addition to setting weekly goals, young children can begin setting long-term goals they will work to achieve over the course of several weeks, months, or years. Figure 4.8 shows a sample goal-setting form for young children who are thinking about their goals for adult life.

Teaching young children to set short-term and long-term goals will benefit them as they continue their journey in becoming expert learners. Expert learners know what they want or need to learn and develop plans for that learning. When we teach young children to set goals, we are helping them gain the skills they need to plan for their own learning.

MOVING FORWARD

We have now discussed all three UDL principles. In this chapter about providing multiple means of action and expression, we considered ways to integrate technology, offer language-based assessments, conduct observations, provide paper-based assessments, and teach young children to set goals. You are armed with a lot of information and, hopefully, many new ideas for supporting all learners in your classroom. Thank you for sticking with me so far! I will meet you in chapter 5 to talk about how to put all of this information together and design lesson plans that use the UDL framework.

Putting It into Action: Designing Lesson Plans in a UDL Framework

Mrs. Boothe has been learning about the Universal Design for Learning framework, and she loves the idea of helping the children in her classroom become expert learners. She is excited to get started but also feels a bit nervous about trying something new and is worried that it might be time consuming to start lesson planning with UDL in mind. So she decides to start small, her first action being adding visual supports to her classroom routines via picture-based checklists. After the children feel comfortable using them, she will add some more choices to classroom activities. Then she will select a third idea to implement. Making changes and additions to her instruction a bit at a time will make the task more manageable and aid her in seeing success from UDL.

Like Mrs. Boothe, you now have an understanding of the UDL framework as it applies in early childhood settings. Over the past four chapters, you have learned the basics of the framework and have been introduced to scenarios in which the three UDL principles were used to support the learning of all young children. Many preschool and kindergarten teachers are already implementing the UDL framework, or components of it, every single day. But you may not be doing everything, or you may be asking yourself how to put all of this information together in a meaningful way that will help children while still being realistic for you to implement in your busy schedule. In this chapter, I walk you through the process of instructional planning for UDL.

REMINDER OF UDL PRINCIPLES

Before we launch into using UDL in lesson planning, I want to quickly remind you of the three principles of Universal Design for Learning that are designed to create expert learners. The first principle is multiple means of engagement. This principle focuses on how we offer various ways for young children to become engaged in and motivated for learning and participation in our classrooms. The second principle is multiple means of representation. When we focus on this principle, we provide instruction using different tools and strategies and, as appropriate, provide the same learning content in a variety of ways. The final UDL principle is multiple means of action and expression, which is how young children show us they have gained knowledge and skills. Figure 5.1 provides a brief reminder of the specific strategies I have discussed for each of these principles. Remember that these are just ideas and not a comprehensive list of ways to use the UDL framework in your classroom.

Figure 5.1

Implementing the UDL Framework

Multiple Means of Engagement
- Providing choice
- Using classroom materials aligned with children's individual interests and cultures
- Offering opportunities to learn with others
- Including hands-on learning activities in the classroom
- Teaching self-monitoring and self-evaluation

Multiple Means of Representation
- Offering a variety of learning materials
- Providing visual supports
- Connecting instruction to previous learning or experiences
- Integrating technology
- Modeling and thinking aloud

Multiple Means of Action and Expression
- Offering language-based assessments
- Conducting observations
- Providing paper-based assessments
- Integrating technology
- Teaching young children to set goals

PLANNING TO USE UDL

When you decide to teach with the UDL framework in mind, don't feel like you need to completely change the way you teach or plan lessons. Choose one small thing and make one change. Master that and then try something new. As you write lesson plans from a UDL perspective, start with your intended learning outcomes for the student and build on that by thinking about ways you already support learners and considering additional strategies that might support diverse learners in your classroom. Remember that the goal of using the UDL framework is enhanced learning. Using the framework itself is not the goal; the UDL framework is simply a method to help you achieve your goal of supporting the learning of all young children.

When I write lesson plans in a UDL framework, I like to use pink, yellow, and blue highlighters, one color for each UDL principle, and highlight ways that I am meeting each principle within my lesson plan. When I first started with UDL, I did this with lessons I had previously taught. By color-coding, I was able to quickly see that I tend to offer multiple means of engagement and representation but frequently provide only one way for learners to demonstrate their knowledge. I took those lesson plans that I had already taught and specifically focused on adding multiple means of action and expression. Over time I have continued to use this highlighter practice (or different colored text if I am writing the lesson plan on my computer). While I am writing the lesson and preparing to teach it, I can see how the lesson supports learners. I am also careful to remember that every single lesson does not have to meet all three UDL principles. As long as each of the three highlighter colors is well represented over the course of a day or a learning unit, I know that I am using the UDL framework to guide instruction. To help you as you think about how to use UDL, I have created a sample lesson plan that uses this framework.

www.redleafpress
.org/cyl/5-2.pdf

Figure 5.2

Sample Lesson Plan for Rhymes

Standard:

Common Core State Standard ELA-Literacy.RF.K.2A: Recognize and produce rhyming words.

Materials needed:

Jack Hartmann video: https://www.youtube.com/watch?v=RVophT8naUM

Hen puppet

Pictures of dog, frog, hog, and log

Lesson Introduction:

Watch Jack Hartmann's YouTube video "I Love to Rhyme" on the class interactive whiteboard.

Teacher says: "We have talked about rhyming before. Remember that when we rhyme, we look for words that have the same ending sound. Who is excited to rhyme with me today?"

Teacher Instruction (I do):

Teacher, while wearing a hen puppet on hand, says: "I would like for you all to meet my special friend. This is Mrs. Hen. Mrs. Hen is here today to help us practice rhymes. She wants to find all of the things in our classroom that rhyme with her name. But, before we can start looking around, I think we need to figure out the ending sound for Mrs. Hen's name. Let's think . . . hen, hen, hen. The beginning sound is *h* (heh) and the next sound is -*en*. So, the ending part of Mrs. Hen's name is -*en*. We need to find words in this room that end with -*en*. Okay, let me see what I have on my desk. I have a book. *Book* ends with -*ook*. That is not the same as -*en*, so Mrs. Hen, you do not rhyme with *book*. Let's try again. But before we move on, I need to take a quick note. Let me grab paper and a pen. Wait . . . *pen*. What sounds does *pen* end with? Let me think. *Pen, pen, pen*. It ends with -*en*. And *hen* ends with -*en*. *Hen, pen*. These rhyme! Mrs. Hen, you rhyme with *pen*! That is so great! I wonder what other words you rhyme with. Let's try looking around the room again. Hmmm . . . *again*. *Again* ends with -*en*. That rhymes with Mrs. Hen! Let's think of other words that rhyme. What about *men, wren, then,* and *den*? So many words rhyme with you, Mrs. Hen!" [Or allow students to supply rhymes.]

Guided Practice (We do):

Teacher: "Well, that was really fun! I loved practicing rhyming with all of you today. Let's do some more! Let me show you a picture. What is on this picture?"

Children: "A dog!"

Teacher: "You are correct. It is a dog. Now we are going to work together to find words that rhyme with *dog*. I have put pictures around the room. Some of the pictures rhyme with *dog* and some do not. Pick a partner and go find one picture that rhymes with *dog*. Bring the picture to me, and we will talk about them together."

The children gather pictures. The teacher holds up the pictures one by one, and the class works together to decide if each word rhymes with *dog*. If the class is incorrect, the teacher uses think-aloud strategies to help the children think through how to determine if it is a rhyming word.

Independent Practice (You do):

Children are given the choice of two assessments for sorting words that rhyme with *cat* and words that do not rhyme with *cat*. Option one is to cut out clip-art pictures from a worksheet and glue each picture into the appropriate column on a worksheet. Option two is to play a sorting game the teacher created on a tablet.

Lesson Closure

As the lesson concludes, Mrs. Hen says goodbye and tells the children all of the words she knows that rhyme with *bye* (*my, hi, try, fly, guy*). She reminds the children that the funny thing about rhyming words is that they sound the same but may not look the same when you spell them.

This lesson includes several of the strategies I have discussed in this book, including providing choice, offering opportunities to learn with others, providing hands-on learning activities, using a variety of learning materials, integrating technology, modeling and thinking aloud, and giving paper-based assessments. This lesson plan may have looked very similar to lessons you teach already. As I have mentioned before, many early childhood teachers are using the UDL framework in their classrooms, even if they don't realize it. And if you are, I encourage you to think of ways that you can use it more, with more intention, and encourage those around you to do so as well.

UDL IN THE CONTEXT OF VARIOUS TEACHING APPROACHES

Depending on the type of school in which you teach, you may be wondering how UDL fits in or how this framework would look in your setting. While I do not promise to know everything about all teaching approaches and I cannot possibly talk about UDL in all types of settings, I do want to offer a brief explanation of how this framework fits into certain settings, specifically Reggio Emilia schools, Charlotte Mason classrooms, and classical education.

The Reggio Emilia approach to early childhood education puts children at the center of learning. Young children's active participation in the learning process is a key feature of the Reggio Emilia approach, and children are encouraged to initiate learning activities and make their own choices about what and how to learn. This approach aligns well with the UDL framework. The Reggio Emilia approach uses hands-on learning activities, discussed in chapter 2 as being one way to engage learners.

A second common early childhood learning approach is the Charlotte Mason classroom. This approach focuses on learning for the sake of learning, and the end goal of instruction is learning, not test scores or academic achievement. This sounds a lot like expert learning to me—what do you think? The Charlotte Mason approach includes UDL strategies we have discussed, such as hands-on learning, language-based learning assessments, and connecting learning to children's interests and experiences.

Finally, classical education is becoming a more popular approach. The classical education approach is designed to provide instruction aligned with children's development. This approach uses language-based assessments and aims to help children understand the tools needed for learning and find their love of knowledge and to provide students tools for learning success. At first glance, it may appear that this approach does not align with the UDL framework, but I believe this initial reaction is incorrect. In many schools, this approach does not often offer choice, so when using the UDL framework within a classical education approach, I recommend offering just two choices and explicitly instructing children how to make decisions about the choices they are offered.

MOVING FORWARD

We have now finished discussing the UDL framework, and I hope that you are feeling prepared to begin implementing the framework and creating expert learners in your own classrooms. Today I challenge you to write one lesson plan with UDL in mind. Think of ways you can offer multiple means of engagement, representation, and action and expression in your classroom. Just like Mrs. Boothe from the beginning of the chapter, pick one small thing to start with. What one simple strategy can you try out in your own classroom this week? When you think about the strategies presented in this book, which one excites you the most? Try it! Plan to make just that one change or addition to your classroom over the next several weeks. Once that becomes habit, choose another simple strategy. Start small and keep adding more ideas—that is how you will effectively implement UDL in your classroom.

Wrapping It Up

Mr. Dorian is passionate about growing and learning in the field of early childhood education. He knows that the more he learns, the better he can support the needs of the young children in his classroom. After learning about the UDL framework, Mr. Dorian is wondering how it can be applied to his own professional learning, so he spends some time explicitly thinking about how each of the three UDL principles can tie to adult learning. In addition, Mr. Dorian considers ways he can use the UDL framework to enhance his professional skills in other aspects of his job, such as teaming with others.

Like Mr. Dorian, you have recently learned a lot about Universal Design for Learning and its applications in preschool and kindergarten classrooms. You know how you can create expert learners by using multiple means of engagement, representation, and action and expression. You have begun to make plans to incorporate the UDL framework into your own instruction (or you are already doing so). Since you may be wondering how else UDL can support you as a teacher, I want to offer two additional ways UDL can be used in your career: collaboration with others and personal professional development.

COLLABORATION WITH FAMILIES

One critical part of being a teacher is teaming with others. Effective teachers do not work alone. We are constantly communicating, collaborating, encouraging, and learning from those around us. And, while working with others makes us better teachers, it can also be challenging, especially when others approach learning and collaborating differently than we do. This is where the UDL framework can support us. We can engage with other professionals and the families of the children in our classroom in a variety of ways.

Early childhood educators communicate with the families of the children in their classroom on a daily (or almost daily) basis. But if your classroom is anything like mine were, those communications are different with every single parent or caregiver. Different families need and want different things from their children's teachers. Some families want daily communication that includes photos, stories, and a minute-by-minute list of what their child did that day. Other families prefer to get a short note once a week that says their child is doing fine. You will also likely have some families who check their email several times an hour, while others may only check email once per week. Some families will rarely (if ever) open their child's take-home folder, but other families will open it every night. The reasons for this are varied and might include cultural beliefs regarding education, families' work and life commitments, or language barriers. As a teacher who approaches collaboration from a UDL framework, you will be prepared to meet the needs of each of these families and all families in between.

So, in practical terms, what does it look like to use a UDL framework when working with families? First, consider the many ways in which you communicate with them. Figure 6.1 offers a list of ways I have seen teachers successfully communicate information to families without a lot of unnecessary effort. For the whole-class communications, you can repeat the same information through many methods: for example, you can paste your newsletter into an email or blog and post on your social media channels with a message something like "Check out what we're doing in Pre-K this week! #MrsLohmannsRockstars #LearningAboutSeasons."

Figure 6.1

Ways to Communicate with Families of Young Children

Communicating with Individual Families	**Communicating with the Class as a Whole**
• Phone calls or text messages	• Printed newsletters
• In-person conversations	• Emails
• Video conference or chat meetings	• Class website/blog
	• Private class page on Facebook, Instagram, etc.
	• Class Twitter feed
	• Smartphone applications for classroom communication

You can also use the UDL framework to offer multiple ways for families to engage in the classroom. The types and levels of classroom involvement that are desired or practical differ for each family, so offering various ways to get involved can ensure that you are meeting everyone's needs. You might offer opportunities for families to come into the classroom to help with parties, read to the class, share about their cultures, or assist with centers. You might offer ways that families can support classroom-wide learning at home by making snacks to bring in, preparing art projects, or going to the public library to check out books for upcoming learning units. You might create optional activities that families complete with their children at home to extend the learning that is happening in the classroom. They key is to offer options and to allow families to select the choice(s) that are best for them.

Family Involvement Varies

When we think about family involvement, it is vital to remember that home-school partnerships look different for each family. Some families get very involved in the classroom while others are less involved. We cannot (and should not) expect that every family is able to volunteer in the classroom or at home. Our job as teachers is to provide opportunities for families to be involved, support involvement, and remain nonjudgmental about families' levels of involvement in our classrooms and schools.

COLLABORATION WITH OTHER EDUCATION PROFESSIONALS

A key influence in how you support young children's learning and development comes through working with other education professionals, including other early childhood teachers, assistant teachers, school administrators, learning specialists, and extracurricular activity providers. In addition, if you are working with young children who receive special education services, you collaborate with medical providers, speech therapists, occupational therapists, physical therapists, and other professionals. As I suspect you have experienced by now, teaming with other professionals requires compromise and finding ways to build on each collaborator's strengths. Each professional collaboration is unique. With this in mind, I recommend approaching these collaborations with a UDL framework.

When you begin a new collaboration, take the time to get to know the other professional (to the extent possible) and explicitly ask them how they prefer to communicate. Some will prefer written communications, while others will want to speak to you either in person or over the phone. While you may find that you are communicating in a variety of ways to meet everyone's preferences, I suspect you will discover that everyone is more responsive to you and you will likely spend less time tracking people down when you use their preferred method.

As a professor who teaches primarily working adults, I have taken a UDL approach to sharing information with my students. When I post information in my online courses, I post it in a basic text format with bullet points. I create infographics and short videos that show the same information so students can select how they want to access it. I also send the information that I post online through the course software as emails. I offer a variety of options for students to contact me, including email, phone calls, text messages, tweets, and online office hours they can attend. While this means that I must be more available to my students, it also means that their needs are met. Similarly, when you use a UDL framework to communicate with other education professionals, it might feel like more work for you, but the results will be worth it.

When considering using the UDL framework to team with colleagues, think about the tasks your team must complete and how you can use each person's personal resources and strengths in completing them. As a classroom teacher, I had a lot of classroom preparation work that had to be done each day, and most days my classroom assistants and I did this work after the children left in the afternoon. Each day, we had to clean up the classroom, set up centers for the following day, make copies of paper-based activities, and fill out any daily reports. On a regular basis, we also had to create bulletin boards, rotate out the classroom library books, and plan upcoming learning units. Any one of the adults in my classroom could complete any of these tasks, but each of us had tasks that were more aligned with our personal preferences and strengths. Through a UDL approach, I attempted to build on each of our strengths and asked my most artistic classroom assistant to create bulletin boards while I completed reports because I like data and reports. But as a team, we were flexible and willing to change our normal tasks to best support each other every day.

Similarly, when I had a coteacher, we took a UDL approach to dividing teaching tasks. We would each teach the lessons that were most aligned with our interests and expertise. But we would also teach each other's content on a regular basis to give the other person time to write lesson plans or engage in professional development activities. Using the UDL framework for collaboration with colleagues involves being flexible and adaptable, with a focus on the skills each professional brings to the collaboration.

PERSONAL PROFESSIONAL DEVELOPMENT

As a teacher, you are expected (and often required for licensure purposes) to continue learning about effective instruction, and you want to do so. But if you are like me (and every early childhood teacher I know), finding the time and the resources for learning can be a challenge. With this in mind, I recommend approaching your own professional development from a UDL framework. This simply means acknowledging that you are an expert learner and you should consider your own preferences and needs by seeking out professional development opportunities that work for you. Your plan may differ from the other teachers in your school, but this is a good thing! When each teacher seeks out professional development that helps them grow, all learners in the school benefit. Figure 6.2 offers a list of questions to ask yourself about your own learning preferences (keep in mind that research has debunked the idea of learning styles, but we do know that learning preferences exist).

www.redleafpress
.org/cyl/6-2.pdf

Figure 6.2

Identifying Your Learning Preferences

- How do I prefer to receive information?

- What do I do during an in-person professional development session? What presenter teaching methods do I prefer?

- How do I behave/act/engage when I attend a webinar?

- What do I do when I listen to an audiobook or podcast?

- What do I do when I read a book?

- Am I comfortable using social media for learning?

- Do I prefer to learn alone or with others?

- What was the best professional development I have experienced?

- What was the worst professional development I have experienced?

- What does my available time look like? When can I participate in professional development?

- What resources do I have to support my professional development (considering the costs of child care, travel, and so on)?

- What are my professional development goals?

To help you out as you consider each question, I have provided my answers to the questions in figure 6.3. Your learning preferences and needs will differ from mine, so your answers may be very different. That is the point of thinking about this—you need to identify what will work best for you! You may also notice that my answers are a bit long. This is good, as the depth provides a solid overview of what I believe is best for me. Remember, though, that as an expert

Figure 6.3

Marla's Learning Preferences

How do I prefer to receive information?

I like to see the information and also do something with it. I prefer to read something or see a visual representation. But I also know that some visual representations make me nauseous (word clouds look so cool, but they overwhelm me and I can't learn anything from them!). I also know that I need to use the information (or at least plan for how to use it) in order to really learn it. "Sit and get" professional development sessions have never worked for me.

What do I do during an in-person professional development session? What presenter teaching methods do I prefer?

It really depends on the topic. Regardless of the topic, I try my best to learn and think about how to apply in my own classroom/career what I am hearing. But I also know that I need to be moving while I am listening to a presenter, so I often kick my leg or chew on my pencil. I suspect some sort of fidget toy would keep my hands busy and help me stay focused, but I have never tried that. I do not like when presenters make us play dumb games, but I do like it when they engage the audience in meaningful discussions and when I leave a professional development with something tangible (like a tool I can use in my classroom or an idea that I can implement immediately without much planning). I don't like it when presenters talk the entire time, but I also don't like it when we spend the entire PD doing activities. I prefer professional development sessions that are a good mix of lectures/presentation and hands-on practice of what we are learning. I also appreciate it when the presenter ensures we get plenty of opportunities to move or to take breaks that allow for movement.

How do I behave/act/engage when I attend a webinar?

I am the world's worst webinar attendee! I love the idea of webinars and I sign up for a bunch of them, but I am horrible about attending them and struggle to sit still and just listen. What seems to work best for me when I attend a webinar is to power walk on the treadmill while watching the webinar on my phone. That meets my need/desire for physical movement and helps me focus. But I cannot take notes on important things I am learning while I am power walking. I need to explore options for taking notes while using the treadmill.

What do I do when I listen to an audiobook or podcast?

Ha ha! I am even worse at audiobooks than I am at webinars. I tune out and start thinking about other things within the first few minutes and miss almost everything that is said. I really want to learn from podcasts because listening while I run or while I am cooking dinner sounds super convenient. I think I should keep trying to learn general information in this manner but never plan for anything auditory to be actual professional development.

What do I do when I read a book?

I love, love, love reading! For learning purposes, I prefer a physical book, but I like ebooks when I am reading fiction stories for fun. When I read a book related to teaching or learning, I like to use sticky notes to indicate things that feel important or meaningful to me. And I love to take handwritten notes about the book so that I can refer to the main points and my takeaways later. The biggest challenge I have with books is finding time to read them. I can't easily multitask while reading, and free time is limited in my day.

Am I comfortable with using social media for learning?

I love social media! Twitter chats and Facebook-based professional development groups are some of my favorite ways to learn. I love (and appreciate) the asynchronous components of social media. In my busy schedule, being able to learn from others on my own time is a huge benefit. I really love that social media means that I get to interact with the experts in many topics that help me grow professionally. Plus, it is free to learn in this manner!

Do I prefer to learn alone or with others?

Hmmm . . . my gut response is that it really depends on what I am learning. But, if I think more deeply about this, I think the true answer is that I like to access the information alone, have time to think it over, and then discuss it with others. But I am picky about the people I learn with. I like to learn with trusted friends who will challenge my ideas, "safe people" so I don't worry about feeling like an idiot with them. I think there are only a handful of people whom I like to learn with. But I know that my learning is deeper when I learn with others instead of trying to learn it all alone.

What was the best professional development I have experienced?

When I was working on my doctorate, my office mate and I had fabulous conversations about many of the articles we were required to read for class. She comes from a different background and had different experiences than I, so we disagreed on many things. But I learned so much from our debates and discussions about the articles we read and other topics relevant to effective instruction. Those conversations were informal but absolutely the best professional development of my career. Even now, ten years after graduation, I have phone calls with her almost weekly where we discuss topics in the field and continue debating how to best support all learners.

What was the worst professional development I have experienced?

Recently, I was in an online book club with a professional organization. There were a lot of us in the book club, so we were assigned to smaller groups.

I was super excited about the book and the prospect of learning how to apply the concepts in my own instruction. But my hopes for the book club did not match the reality. The people in my assigned group were at a different stage in their career than I, and what we all needed from the book club was different. Eventually, I dropped out of the club and just read the book on my own. I discussed the book via text with other colleagues who had been assigned to different groups and loved that.

What does my available time look like? When can I participate in professional development?

As a busy working mom of four, my time is limited. I want to spend hours every week engaged in professional development, but that is just not feasible. I need easy-to-understand professional development sessions that I can complete while doing other things. I want ideas that can be implemented without much effort on my part. Asynchronous professional development seems to be the most practical for me, but occasional daytime learning opportunities are also an option. The problem is that if I do spend part of a workday in a professional development, I need to find time to complete the work that I would normally have done that day.

What resources do I have to support my professional development (considering the costs of child care, travel, and so on)?

I have a professional development budget to attend conferences and webinars. I can ask for books as Christmas and birthday gifts from my family. Finding child care for an in-person professional development session outside of my traditional working hours is challenging. I would need to hire a babysitter or ensure that my husband is not traveling for work that week.

What are my professional development goals?

My professional goal is to never stop learning and growing as a teacher. I want to learn more every day about how to best support teachers in meeting the needs of all learners. This means that I need to keep learning about adult learning and the best practices in teaching children. I want to be a better teacher every day, and I want the "me" five years from now to be a much better teacher than I am today! Right now, I am especially interested in learning more about addressing equity issues in the classroom.

learner, I am willing to try different things to find out what might be most appropriate for me.

Now that you have considered both your learning preferences and your learning needs, let's use that information to think about designing your own professional development plan. As I look over my answers to the questions, I notice several key things: (1) I want to keep learning, (2) my time is limited, (3) I like to reflect on learning with others, and (4) books and social media seem to be some of my preferred ways to access learning. Because I enjoy seeing visual representations of content (and just because it is fun), I recommend creating a picture of yourself as a learner. It does not need to be fancy, but it can help you better understand what you need and want from your professional development. If images are not your preference, you can instead create a table or an audio recording discussing your preferences. My (very basic and not pretty) self-portrait can be seen in figure 6.4. Please don't laugh at my drawing skills!

With my self-portrait in mind, I developed both a short-term and a long-term plan for increasing my own learning as a teacher. My current professional development plan for this semester is to read *Multiplication Is for White People* by Lisa Delpit and *Teaching across Cultural Strengths* by Alicia Fedelina Chávez and Susan Diana Longerbeam, follow the authors of these books on Twitter, and ask some of my trusted colleagues to read the books as well so that we can discuss them via text message or Zoom sessions. I would love to read more than just two books and focus on learning in several topics, but this is not realistic for me right now. And it is important that we create a professional development plan that will lead to success for us and improved outcomes for our students.

Take some time to create your own professional development plan. What do you want (or need) to learn in the coming months, and how will you learn it? If you are required to have continuing education hours for your teaching license, be sure that your plan includes activities that will provide these for you. Make sure to be realistic in what you plan. Remember that you can always add more professional development activities to your list once you complete the initial ones.

Figure 6.4

Self-Portrait as an Expert Learner

CONCLUSION

I have enjoyed spending time with you, and I sincerely hope you have enjoyed learning about the Universal Design for Learning framework and how it may be used in your classroom and school. Over the past few chapters, you have learned the basics of the UDL framework, how to ensure that you have multiple means of engagement, representation, and action and expression in your classroom and in your interactions with others. But remember, this is just the beginning. As a lifelong learner, you should keep learning and growing in your expertise. There is so much more to learn about UDL than what I could possibly share with you in this book. I am still constantly learning myself! I hope that we will see each other soon in a UDL webinar or Twitter chat. At the end of this chapter, I offer a list of resources that I highly recommend for more specific information about implementing the UDL framework in early childhood classrooms.

As you work to implement what you have learned, remember a few key points:

- There is not one way to "do UDL." In fact, I remember hearing Dr. David Rose say in a webinar years ago that anyone who says they are "doing UDL" does not understand the framework. One of the most beautiful things about UDL is that it is simply a framework that you adapt to meet your needs and the needs of your classroom, curriculum, and students.

- Start with one change or addition. You cannot do it all at once, and you should not try to do so!

- The key to using the UDL framework is being proactive in your planning. As you prepare lessons and activities, consider what you want young children to learn. Plan your lessons with flexibility based on the end result. I love the phrase "begin with the end in mind," and this is how I recommend approaching UDL. Think about what strategies you can implement that will help the children in your classroom achieve the desired result.

- Expert learners want to learn and are constantly learning from the experiences and people around them. The UDL framework supports both you and your students in becoming expert learners.

Thank you for joining me over the past six chapters. As you implement the UDL framework in your classroom, please let me know how it is going. Tweet photos or stories to me at @MarlaLohmann. I love hearing about your experiences! Good luck moving forward!

Articles for Learning More about UDL in Preschool

Deborah Chen and Jamie Dote-Kwan, "Preschoolers with Visual Impairments and Additional Disabilities: Using Universal Design for Learning and Differentiation," *Young Exceptional Children* 24 (2): 70–81. https://doi.org/10.1177%2F1096250620922205.

Ariane N. Gauvreau, Marla J. Lohmann, and Katrina A. Hovey, "Circle Is for Everyone: Using UDL to Promote Inclusion during Circle Times," *Young Exceptional Children* (July 2021). https://doi.org/10.1177%2F10962506211028576.

Ariane N. Gauvreau, Marla J. Lohmann, and Katrina A. Hovey, "Using a Universal Design for Learning Framework to Provide Multiple Means of Representation in the Early Childhood Classroom," *Journal of Special Education Apprenticeship* 8, no. 1 (2019): art. 3.

Marla J. Lohmann, Katrina A. Hovey, and Ariane N. Gauvreau, "Using a Universal Design for Learning Framework to Enhance Engagement in the Early Childhood Classroom," *Journal of Special Education Apprenticeship* 7 (2): art. 5.

Howard Parette Jr. and Craig Blum, "Using Flexible Participation in Technology-Supported, Universally Designed Preschool Activities," *Teaching Exceptional Children* 46 (January 2014): 60–67. https://doi.org/10.1177%2F004005991404600307.

Nancy S. Stockall, Lindsay Dennis, and Melinda Miller. "Right from the Start: Universal Design for Preschool," *Teaching Exceptional Children* 45 (1): 10–17. https://doi.org/10.1177%2F004005991204500103.

Discussion Questions

CHAPTER 1

1. When you talk about people with disabilities, do you prefer to use person-first or identity-first language? Why?
2. How do you define the term *equity*? What does equity look like in your classroom?
3. The chapter talks about people pushing strollers on wheelchair ramps. What other universally designed supports do you use on a regular basis?
4. Why is proactive instructional planning important?
5. How would you define an expert learner? What characteristics do you think an expert learner embodies?
6. Can you think of someone you know whom you would describe as an expert learner? What makes you see them this way?
7. In your own words, how would you describe the UDL framework as a whole?

CHAPTER 2

1. What is your typical response to children who do not appear to be engaged in classroom learning?
2. Why is children's motivation critical for learning?
3. What is one new way you can offer choice in your own classroom? What challenges do you foresee in offering this choice? How might choice benefit the children in your classroom?
4. What are some of the interests of the children in your classroom? What is one way you can connect classroom instruction to those interests?
5. What is one way you can connect classroom instruction to the cultures, strengths, and abilities represented in your classroom and community?
6. How do you feel about working with others? In what ways does collaborative learning motivate you as a learner?

7. Consider the types of activities listed in figure 2.4. Which of these could you use in your classroom to provide opportunities for collaborative learning?

8. What is one way that you currently use hands-on learning in your classroom? How else can you incorporate this strategy into classroom instruction?

9. How do you evaluate yourself? Think about how you ensure that you are completing required work and personal tasks and meeting other expectations in your life as well as how you evaluate your own teaching effectiveness.

10. What long-term benefits result from teaching children to self-monitor?

11. How will you teach self-evaluation in your own classroom?

12. In your own words, how would you describe the UDL principle of multiple means of engagement?

CHAPTER 3

1. What is the most common way you present learning material in your classroom? Which means of representation is your go-to strategy?

2. This chapter mentions that learning styles are a myth. What did you think when you read this? What is your experience with the idea of learning styles?

3. Think about the scenario about Miss Franklin and her use of various learning materials. Select one upcoming activity in your classroom and explain how you can use a variety of materials in teaching that lesson.

4. Select one classroom material and explain how you can use it for another instructional purpose (for example, using puppets to help teach science concepts).

5. If you were to add visual supports to one daily classroom routine, which routine would you choose? What steps are part of this routine? What images would be appropriate for each of these steps?

6. Think about your current classroom learning topics. How do you connect current learning to young children's previous experiences and knowledge? What is one new strategy you can try?

7. How do you currently use technology in your classroom? In what other ways might technology tools enhance children's learning?

8. Why is it important to use technology with intentionality?

9. What do you believe are the biggest drawbacks to integrating technology in early childhood classrooms?

10. How might you use the idea of modeling and thinking aloud in your classroom?

11. How do you, as a learner, benefit when someone models a new skill for you?

12. In your own words, how would you describe the UDL principle of multiple means of representation?

CHAPTER 4

1. Generally, how do you assess young children's learning? What are the benefits to this method? What are the drawbacks?

2. Why is ongoing (often referred to as formative) assessment vital in the early childhood classroom? How do you use these assessments to guide daily instructional planning?

3. What language-based assessments do you currently use? In what other ways can you use oral language to assess young children's learning?

4. Why are observations of young children important?

5. When you conduct observations, what do you normally look for?

6. How can you ensure that your personal biases do not influence what you record during observations?

7. Paper-based assessments are commonly used in many classrooms. How do you currently use paper-based assessments in your instruction? What additional ways can you do this?

8. Share one way that you can use technology to assess learning in your classroom.

9. How do you set goals in your own life? How does goal setting help you?

10. Why is it important for all learners, including young children, to set goals for themselves?

11. How can you incorporate goal setting into your classroom?

12. In your own words, how would you describe the UDL principles of multiple means of action and expression?

CHAPTER 5

1. How are you feeling about the UDL framework at this point?
2. This chapter talks about using the "I do, we do, you do" format when writing lesson plans. How do you write lesson plans?
3. One point that has been mentioned throughout the book is to start small and choose one strategy to implement and master before adding another strategy. In your lesson planning this week, what strategy will you try? Why did you select that strategy?
4. At this point in the book and in your own words, how would you describe the UDL framework as a whole?

CHAPTER 6

1. How can you take a UDL approach to communicating with families?
2. How will you offer a variety of ways for families to participate in your classroom and team with you?
3. Thinking about your current colleagues, how can the UDL framework increase your team effectiveness? What would a UDL approach look like for you and your colleagues?
4. Look at figure 6.2 and identify your own learning preferences. How would you describe yourself as a learner? Consider drawing a self-portrait of yourself as a learner (see figure 6.4 for an example of this), doing an audio recording in which you describe your learning preferences, or creating a table or other text-based representation.
5. What is your personal professional development plan?
6. How do you see the UDL framework aligning (or not aligning) with your school's teaching approach?
7. As you conclude this book, how would you describe an expert learner? How has your definition changed?
8. What do you believe all early childhood educators should know about the UDL framework?

References

Aguirre-Munoz, Zenaida, and Michelle L. Pantoya, 2016. "Engineering Literacy and Engagement in Kindergarten Classrooms." *Journal of Engineering Education* 105 (4): 630–54. https://doi.org/10.1002/jee.20151.

Ainley, Mary. 2006. "Connecting with Learning: Motivation, Affect and Cognition in Interest Processes." *Educational Psychology Review* 18 (4): 391–405. https://doi.org/10.1007/s10648-006-9033-0.

Alanís, Iliana. 2018. "Enhancing Collaborative Learning: Activities and Structures in a Dual Language Preschool Classroom." *Association of Mexican American Educators Journal* 12 (1): 4–26. https://doi.org/10.24974/amae.12.1.375.

Altermatt, Ellen Rydell, Eva M. Pomerantz, Diane N. Ruble, Karin S. Frey, and Faith Knesz Greulich. 2002. "Predicting Changes in Children's Self-Perceptions of Academic Competence: A Naturalistic Examination of Evaluative Discourse among Classmates." *Developmental Psychology* 38 (6): 903–17. https://doi.org/10.1037/0012-1649.38.6.903.

Andrieux, Mathieu, and Luc Proteau. 2016. "Observational Learning: Tell Beginners What They Are about to Watch and They Will Learn Better." *Frontiers in Psychology* 7, art. 51. https://doi.org/10.3389/fpsyg.2016.00051.

Bergman, Daniel, and Jason Morphew. 2014. "Comparing Classroom Interactive Behaviors of Science and Non-Science Pre-Service Teachers." *Journal of Classroom Interaction* 49 (2): 4–10.

CAST. 2018. "The UDL Guidelines." Version 2.2. http://udlguidelines.cast.org.

Centre for Excellence in Universal Design. 2020. *What Is Universal Design?* https://universaldesign.ie/what-is-universal-design.

Cohrssen, Caroline, Ben De Quadros-Wander, Jane Page, and Suzana Klarin. 2017. "Between the Big Trees: A Project-Based Approach to Investigating Shape and Spatial Thinking in a Kindergarten Program." *Australasian Journal of Early Childhood* 42 (March 1): 94–104. https://doi.org/10.23965%2FAJEC.42.1.11.

Conn-Powers, Michael, Alice Frazeur Cross, Elizabeth Krider Traub, and Lois Hutter-Pishgahi. 2006. "The Universal Design of Early Education: Moving Forward for All Children." *Beyond the Journal.* https://fpg.unc.edu/sites/fpg.unc.edu/files/resources/presentations-and-webinars/ConnPowersBTJ%281%29.pdf.

Couse, Leslie J., and Dora W. Chen. 2010. "A Tablet Computer for Young Children? Exploring Its Viability for Early Childhood Education." *Journal of Research on Technology in Education* 43 (1): 75–98.

DEC and NAEYC (Division for Early Childhood/National Association for the Education of Young Children). 2009. "Early Childhood Inclusion: A Joint Position Statement of the Division for Early Childhood (DEC) and the National Association for the Education of Young Children (NAEYC)." Chapel Hill: University of North Carolina, FPG Child Development Institute.

Deci, Edward L., and Richard M. Ryan. 2012. "Self-Determination Theory." In *Handbook of Theories of Social Psychology*, edited by Paul A. M. Van Lange, Arie W. Kruglanski, and E. Tory Higgins, 416–36. London: Sage Publications. https://psycnet.apa.org/doi/10.4135/9781446249215.n21.

Division for Early Childhood. 2014. "DEC Recommended Practices in Early Intervention/Early Childhood Special Education 2014." www.dec-sped.org /recommendedpractices.

Dowd, Amy Jo, and Bo Stjerne Thomsen. 2021. *Learning through Play: Increasing Impact, Reducing Inequality.* The Lego Foundation. https://cms.learningthrough play.com/media/jxgbzwos/learning-through-play-increasing-impact_reducing -inequality_white-paper.pdf.

Elimelech, Adi, and Dorit Aram. 2019. "A Digital Early Spelling Game: The Role of Auditory and Visual Support." *AERA Open* 5 (2): 1–11. https://doi.org/10.1177 %2F2332858419857702.

Elliott, Ceri, and Karola Dillenburger. 2016. "The Effect of Choice on Motivation for Young Children on the Autism Spectrum during Discrete Trial Teaching." *Journal of Research in Special Educational Needs* 16 (3): 187–98. https://doi .org/10.1111/1471-3802.12073.

Espinosa, Linda M. 2013. *Early Education for Dual Language Learners: Promoting School Readiness and Early School Success.* National Center on Immigrant Integration Policy, Migration Policy Institute. www.migrationpolicy.org/sites/default /files/publications/COI-EspinosaFINAL.pdf.

Ganz, Jennifer B., and Margaret M. Flores. 2010. "Supporting the Play of Preschoolers with Autism Spectrum Disorders: Implementation of Visual Scripts." *Young Exceptional Children* 13 (2): 58–70.

Gauvreau, Ariane N. 2019. "Using 'Snack Talk' to Support Social Communication in Inclusive Preschool Classrooms." *Young Exceptional Children* 22 (4): 187–97. https://doi.org/10.1177%2F1096250617725503.

Gauvreau, Ariane N., Marla J. Lohmann, and Katrina A. Hovey. 2019. "Using a Universal Design for Learning Framework to Provide Multiple Means of Representation in the Early Childhood Classroom." *Journal of Special Education Apprenticeship* 8 (1): art. 3. https://scholarworks.lib.csusb.edu/josea/vol8/iss1/3.

Gauvreau, Ariane N., and Ilene S. Schwartz. 2013. "Using Visual Supports to Increase the Appropriate Behavior of Young Children with Autism." In *Young Exceptional*

Child Monograph No. 15: Addressing Young Children's Challenging Behavior, edited by Michaelene M. Ostrosky and Susan R. Sandall. Los Angeles: Division for Early Childhood.

Glass, Don, Anne Meyer, and David H. Rose. 2013. "Universal Design for Learning and the Arts." *Harvard Educational Review* 83 (1): 98–119. https://psycnet.apa.org/doi/10.17763/haer.83.1.33102p26478p54pw.

Green, Katherine B., Nicole M. Mays, and Kristine Jolivette. 2020. "Making Choices: A Proactive Way to Improve Behaviors for Young Children with Challenging Behaviors." *Beyond Behavior* 20 (1): 25–31.

Green, Vanessa A., Tessa Prior, Emily Smart, Tanya Boelema, Heather Drysdale, Susan Harcourt, Laura Roche, and Hannah Waddington. 2017. "The Use of Individualized Video Modeling to Enhance Positive Peer Interactions in Three Preschool Children." *Education & Treatment of Children* 40 (3): 353–78. https://psycnet.apa.org/doi/10.1353/etc.2017.0015.

Halle, Tamara, Nicole Forry, Elizabeth C. Hair, Kate Perper, Laura D. Wandner, Julia Wessel, and Jessica Vick. 2009. "Disparities in Early Learning and Development: Lessons from the Early Childhood Longitudinal Study, Birth Cohort (ECLS-B)." Child Trends. June. https://www.childtrends.org/publications/disparities-in-early-learning-and-development-lessons-from-the-early-childhood-longitudinal-study-birth-cohorts-ecls-b-2.

Helton, Maria. R., and Sheila R. Alber-Morgan. 2020. "Improving Young Children's Behavior with GAMES: Group Contingency Approaches for Managing Elementary-Classroom Settings." *Young Exceptional Children* 23, no. 1 (March): 24–35. https://doi.org/10.1177%2F1096250618798340.

Howard, Eboni C. 2015. "What Matters Most for Children: Influencing Inequality at the Start of Life." American Institutes for Research. www.air.org/sites/default/files/downloads/report/Early-Childhood-Education-Equity-Howard-August-2015.pdf.

Iyengar, Sheena S., and Mark R. Lepper. 2000. "When Choice Is Demotivating: Can One Desire Too Much of a Good Thing?" *Journal of Personality and Social Psychology* 79 (6): 995–1006.

Jolivette, Kristine, Katherine McCormick, Lee Ann Jung, and Amy Shearer Lingo. 2004. "Embedding Choices into the Daily Routines of Young Children with Behavior Problems: Eight Reasons to Build Social Competence." *Beyond Behavior* 13 (3): 21–26.

Juergensen, Rachel, and Elizabeth Rae Thomas. 2019. "Universal Design for Learning and Multi-tiered Systems of Support: Current Questions, Concerns, and Potential Steps Forward from the Field of Special Education." *Director* 39 (4): 6–8.

Kim, Sun Mi, Sung Yong Park, Young In Kim, Young Don Son, Un-Sun Chung, Kyung Joon Min, and Doug Hyun Han. 2016. "Affective Network and Default Mode

Network in Depressive Adolescents with Disruptive Behaviors." *Neuropsychiatric Disease and Treatment* 12 (December 31): 49–56. https://doi.org/10.2147/NDT .S95541.

Levy, Sharona. 2013. "Young Children's Learning of Water Physics by Constructing Working Systems." *International Journal of Technology & Design Education* 23 (3): 537–66. http://dx.doi.org/10.1007/s10798-012-9202-z.

Lohmann, Marla. J. 2021. *Positive Behavior Interventions and Supports for Preschool and Kindergarten.* St. Paul, MN: Redleaf Press.

Lohmann, Marla J., Katrina A. Hovey, and Ariane N. Gauvreau. 2018. "Using a Universal Design for Learning Framework to Enhance Engagement in the Early Childhood Classroom." *Journal of Special Education Apprenticeship* 7 (2): art. 5.

Malec, Alesia, Shelley Stagg Peterson, and Heba Elsherief. 2017. "Assessing Young Children's Oral Language: Recommendations for Classroom Practice and Policy." *Canadian Journal of Education* 40 (3): 362–92.

Marzano, Robert J. 2004. "The Developing Vision of Vocabulary Instruction." In *Vocabulary Instruction: Research to Practice*, edited by James F. Baumann and Edward J. Kame'enui, 100–117. New York: Guilford Press.

Master, Allison, Sapna Cheryan, and Andrew N. Meltzoff. 2017. "Social Group Membership Increases STEM Engagement among Preschoolers." *Developmental Psychology* 53 (2): 201–9. https://psycnet.apa.org/record/2016-42715-001.

Meadan, Hedda, Michaelene M. Ostrosky, Brooke Triplett, Amanda Michna, and Angel Fettig. 2011. "Using Visual Supports with Young Children with Autism Spectrum Disorder." *Teaching Exceptional Children* 43 (6): 28–35.

Meyer, Anne, David H. Rose, and David Gordon. 2014. *Universal Design for Learning: Theory and Practice.* Wakefield, MA: CAST Professional Publishing.

Muench, Frederick. 2010. "The Burden of Choice." *Psychology Today* (blog). www .psychologytoday.com/us/blog/more-tech-support/201011/the-burden-choice.

NAEYC (National Association for the Education of Young Children). 2020. *Professional Standards and Competencies for Early Childhood Educators.* www.naeyc .org/resources/position-statements/professional-standards-competencies.

———. 2022. *Developmentally Appropriate Practice in Early Childhood Programs: Serving Children from Birth through Age 8.* 4th ed. Washington, DC: NAEYC.

———. n.d. "DAP: Observing, Documenting, and Assessing Children's Development and Learning." www.naeyc.org/resources/position-statements/dap/assessing -development.

NAEYC (National Association for the Education of Young Children) and the Fred Rogers Center for Early Learning and Children's Media. 2012. "Technology and Interactive Media as Tools in Early Childhood Programs Serving Children from

Birth through Age 8." www.naeyc.org/sites/default/files/globally-shared /downloads/PDFs/resources/position-statements/ps_technology.pdf.

Nancekivell, Shaylene E., Priti Shah, and Susan A. Gelman. 2020. "Maybe They're Born with It, or Maybe It's Experience: Toward a Deeper Understanding of the Learning Style Myth." *Journal of Educational Psychology* 112 (2): 221–35. http:// dx.doi.org/10.1037/edu0000366.

Naylor, Anna Schmidt, Deborah Kamps, and Howard Wills. 2018. "The Effects of the CW-FIT Group Contingency on Class-Wide and Individual Behavior in an Urban First Grade Classroom." *Education & Treatment of Children* 41 (4): 1–30. https:// psycnet.apa.org/doi/10.1353/etc.2018.0000.

Perels, Franziska, Miriam Merget-Kullmann, Milena Wende, Bernhard Schmitz, and Carla Buchbinder. 2009. "Improving Self-Regulated Learning of Preschool Children: Evaluation of Training for Kindergarten Teachers." *British Journal of Educational Psychology* 79 (2): 311–27. https://psycnet.apa.org/doi/10.1348 /000709908X322875.

Philippakos, Zoi A. Traga. 2020. "Developing Strategic Learners: Supporting Self-Efficacy through Goal Setting and Reflection." *Language and Literacy Spectrum* 30 (1): art. 1.

Pokorski, Elizabeth A. 2019. "Group Contingencies to Improve Classwide Behavior of Young Children." *Teaching Exceptional Children* 51, no. 5 (May): 340–49. https:// doi.org/10.1177%2F0040059919835438.

Rittle-Johnson, Bethany, Emily Fyfe, Laura E. McLean, and Katherine L. McEldoon. 2013. "Emerging Understanding of Patterning in 4-Year-Olds." *Journal of Cognition and Development* 14 (3): 376–96. https://doi.org/10.1080/15248372.2012.689897.

Roche, Leigh. 2018. "The Power of Choice for Toddlers: A Rationale for Implementing Choice Theory in the Early Childhood Classroom." *International Journal of Choice Theory & Reality Therapy* 37 (2): 50–55.

Scott, Catherine. 2010. "The Enduring Appeal of 'Learning Styles.'" *Australian Journal of Education* 54 (1): 5–17.

Simmons, Paul. 2020. "The Evolution of Universal Design: A Win-Win Concept for All." https://rockymountainada.org/news/blog/evolution-universal-design -win-win-concept-all.

Van Kleeck, Anne. 2008. "Proving Preschool Foundations for Later Reading Comprehension: The Importance of and Ideas for Targeting Inferencing in Storybook-Sharing Interventions." *Psychology in the Schools* 45 (7): 627–43.

Wiggins, Grant, and Jay McTighe. 2005. *Understanding by Design.* 2nd ed. Alexandria, VA: Association for Supervision & Curriculum Development.

Index